Highlights from Dean Wiltse's Career

Greenfield Online, Inc. Announces New Chief Executive Officer

By Kurt Peters, Digital Commerce, May 4, 2001

Dean Wiltse becomes Chief Executive Officer of Greenfield Online, Inc., a leading global Internet-based marketing research and business intelligence firm.

Greenfield Online files for initial public offering worth up to $75 million

By Jeff Miller, Boston Business Journal, July 5, 2004

Greenfield Online Inc., an online market research survey company based in Wilton, Conn., recently set the price range for its proposed IPO at $13 to $15 per share, according to its filings with the Securities and Exchange Commission.

If the company were to go out at the upper end of its range, the IPO would be worth $75 million.

The company plans to issue 4 million new shares and to sell 1 million shares currently owned by investors and management.

For the first seven years of its life, Greenfield derived most of its revenue from custom survey work. In 2002, however, Greenfield dedicated itself to Internet-based surveys for market research.

Since then, revenues have grown substantially. For fiscal year 2003, Greenfield reported $25.9 million in revenue, a 79 percent increase over 2002. Greenfield also swung to a profit in 2003, posting $1.6 million in net income.

For the first three months of 2004, Greenfield made $8.6 million in revenue, an 88 percent increase over the first three months of 2003, and made $325,000 in net income, 7 percent less than it did in the first quarter of last year.

The company has also seen its headcount quadruple over the past two years. In February 2002, the company employed 54 people. By May 2004 that number had grown to 216.

"And the Survey Says... Solutions"

By Colin Beasty, (former) Associate Editor, CRM, June 20, 2006

Investment firm Austin Ventures bought Perseus Development and WebSurveyor Corporation for an undisclosed amount today. It will combine the two companies into a single entity that will be led by Dean Wiltse, former CEO of Greenfield Online. Wiltse will become chairman and CEO of the new company. The acquisition and resulting technology integration will create a full "suite" of surveying solutions for its customers, according to Wiltse. "Depending upon their needs, it's great for customers. They can start at the departmental level with a tool like WebSurveyor, and then move up to an enterprise-wide platform from Perseus. We're seeing a lot of customers making that jump up to an EFM solution." Esteban Kolsky, research director at Gartner, agrees with Wiltse, and says both brands "are a perfect complement to one another. Both of these companies were leaders at what they did. Combining them makes perfect sense."

Thumbspeak Ranked as Number 1 Free Business Application at iTunes

Scottsdale, AZ (PRWEB) October 19, 2010

Thumbspeak LLC announces that its revolutionary new business application was ranked number one at iTunes on Monday, October 18, 2010.

Thumbspeak's do-it yourself (DIY) Mobile Relationship Marketing platform and highly interactive application enable businesses to connect with audiences in real-time via their smart phones. "Thumbspeak is the perfect way to connect with your customer and prospects on their smart phones! They want to provide feedback and stay connected. Businesses can build loyalty by giving them a voice. Mobile connectivity is pervasive and your business will benefit by getting valuable insights and encouraging advocacy," said Thumbspeak's Founder and CEO Dean Wiltse. Questions are easily entered through our intuitive, easy to use web interface and sent to specific smart phone users. The audience enjoys responding because it lets them shape the products and services they care about and our mobile platform makes it fast and fun.

Mobile Research Platform Thumbspeak Sold to Cint

By Brian Tarran, Research Live, February 8, 2011

Wiltse launched Thumbspeak and its iPhone app in July last year, and Android and Blackberry versions of the app are said to be "just days away from hitting the mobile market".

Users of the app have to create an account and answer a series of attribute questions before they can start taking surveys, and Thumbspeak clients can use this data to target questions at specific types of users.

Recent revisions to the app have added functionality to enable private, company-branded groups, while introducing the ability for users to manage their profile and update them with additional information to aid the targeting process. Indeed, Wiltse said the app now presents users with the same profile questions asked of panellists within the Cint Panel Exchange (CPX), a sample-buying marketplace.

FoodLogiQ welcomes new CEO Dean Wiltse

Durham, N.C., Sept. 10, 2015 /PRNewswire

FoodLogiQ, the leading food safety, traceability and sustainability Software as a Service company, today announced that the company has expanded its most recent round of growth financing. These additional funds will be used to accelerate the development and introduction of its industry leading product suite and to further build out its leadership team to take the business to the next level.

In addition to this round of investment, FoodLogiQ is thrilled to welcome Dean Wiltse as the organization›s new Chief Executive Officer (CEO), effective September 1, 2015. "Dean brings an immense wealth of knowledge in this space needed to expand on this growth."

The 25 Most Innovative Ag-Tech Startups

By Maggie McGrath and Chloe Sorvino, Forbes Magazine, June 28, 2017

When our nation was founded 241 years ago, farming was the economy's primary driver. By 1870, nearly half of the employed population held jobs in agriculture. Today, it's a $3 trillion industry - but only 2% of Americans hold a farm-oriented job.

This is, in many ways, thanks to technology. Tractors and other automation advances in the 20th century let large farms shift management to only a handful of people. But this, paradoxically, has also slowed things down in the 21st. With only a few people working every farm, there's not a lot of time - or incentive - to innovate.

To find the 25 ag-tech startups that carry the most potential, we surveyed the agricultural technology landscape by speaking with experts, venture capitalists and accelerators; then, we examined financials and each company's agricultural credentials. A special thanks goes to Seana Day at the Mixing Bowl for her comprehensive research on the ag-tech environment.

FoodLogiQ: The average food recall costs companies $10 million. FoodLogiQ aims to reduce those costs by using data to track a supply chain (i.e, food) from the farm to the fork, ensuring the correct foods are recalled. *Ag cred:* Works with more than 3,500 food companies, including Whole Foods, Subway, and Chipotle.

FoodLogiQ Secures $19.5M in Oversubscribed Financing Round

Business Wire, March 29, 2018

"The substantial amount of investment interest FoodLogiQ has received is indicative of the confidence in our amazing team and the value of our product to our customers and the food industry," said Dean Wiltse, CEO of FoodLogiQ. "It is great validation to know that we're moving in the right direction and fulfilling our mission of mapping the world's food chain."

Amazing Success

During Economic Crisis

Amazing Success

During Economic Crisis

Strategic Leadership Advice for Every Entrepreneur

Dean Wiltse

ISBN: 978-0-578-76544-0

Cover design by Alison Shoemaker
Interior design by HMDpublishing
Edited by Barry Lyons

Printed in the United States of America

First Edition

To my mother, Marguerite Fontanella Wiltse

Your strength and love has been an inspiration to your children, grandchildren and all that have been fortunate to know you. I love you from the depths of my heart.

Contents

FOREWORD

The rule of thumb defining a recession is two quarters of negative GDP growth. The Gross Domestic Product (GDP) is the market value of all final goods and services produced within a country in a given period of time.

The United States of America has experienced two recessions during the last twenty years and as of this writing is in the midst of a third recession.

Greenfield Online had incurred net losses of $52.6 million; $17.3 million of that was lost during 2000 and 2001. I joined as CEO in March of 2001, which was about a year after the dotcom bubble burst. Those were some of the most difficult economic times in our country's history and is now referred to as the early 2000s recession. Unemployment reached a high of 6.3% in June of 2003. We survived those times and went on to flourish. By 2003, we were profitable and growing rapidly. In 2004 we went public on NASDAQ and used the trading symbol of SRVY.

My next CEO position began the end of 2005 with Austin Ventures, weeks after I left my position as CEO of Greenfield Online. I joined their "CEO in waiting" program, which was designed to identify businesses to acquire, put in an experienced CEO, grow the business, and get a return on the money invested through an eventual sale of the company. Together, we identified two small companies, Perseus and Websurveyor. Austin Ventures acquired both of them, merged them into one company, and called the new company Vovici. The acquisitions and merger happened during 2006.

The next major economic downturn for the economy occurred only six years after the last economic collapse, from December 2007 until

June 2009. This horrible downturn, now referred to as The Great Recession, had implications not just for the United States economy but also for the world. This recession lasted one year and six months, with unemployment hitting a high of 10% in October of 2009.

Vovici survived that economic downturn too and went on to flourish. The company was eventually sold in July of 2011 for seventy-six million dollars (the original investment to buy Perseus and Websurveyor was under fifteen million dollars).

In February of 2020 the United States and global economies suffered yet another crisis with the dawn of the COVID-19 pandemic, only ten years after the last recession, and this pandemic is still going on as of this writing. Unemployment reached 14.7% during April of 2020.

As Einstein put it, "Crisis brings progress." Now is the time to reinvent the way we do business and take a competitive position in the market.

This is my story of the days I served as CEO during these very difficult economic times and how each company survived. I hope this book is helpful to others in business—and useful when the business climate takes a turn for the worst.

ACKNOWLEDGMENTS

My wife Stefie and I have been together for the last seven years. She is my hero. Her story in life has been an inspiration to me. She was abandoned as an infant on the street. Her new, now-deceased sister found her, brought her home, and kept her in a closet for safekeeping until discovered by the rest of the family living in the house. They adopted Stefie and made her their sister. I have fallen in love with this powerful, strong-willed woman and dedicate this book to her. Thank you to Stefie's family for "adopting" me recently too, and thank you Stefie for allowing me into your life and building a family with me. You have so much love for your family.

I must thank my mother and father. They provided me with a wonderful childhood, education, a loving home, and the confidence to do whatever I wanted to do. There was a drive instilled in me ever since I was a child to be my own boss and make decisions based on my core values and instincts.

To my baby sister, Linda, who is also a schoolteacher and a writer. I love you Bill, Julia, and Anna. My older brother, Bob, is now the center of our family and together with Evie, Bob's better half. They care for our mother while he runs his own real estate business. The Fontanellas, my mother's family, were entrepreneurs. My Dad's family too, the Wiltses. Salvatore Fontanella, came to the United States in 1921 from Piscara, Italy, with my grandmother, Linda. They entered through Ellis Island. He started as a bandleader in the Catskills, opened a dry cleaner, and eventually purchased a small apartment building in Catskill, New York. I think I got my entrepreneurial spirit from him. On my Dad's side his grandfather owned and operated the Wiltse Ice Company in the 1920s in upstate New York.

Thank you to my three sons Adam, Luke, and Joshua. I am so proud of each of you and have always loved you. You have always been in my thoughts and prayers. Alex, Valentina, and Alessandro, I hope to be the best father I can be.

INTRODUCTION

B efore I begin to take you on my journey as a first time CEO, I want to tell you why I believe the Board of Directors of Greenfield Online may have recruited me. I can't tell you for sure, but my guess now, looking back, was that because the situation was so dire no other candidate would say "yes." You might think that can't be true, but the situation was dire and they saw something in me as opposed to other candidates. I was flattered to realize that I was selected as the person to turn things around, to determine the strategy, keep the right products and the people—and to keep the company viable.

So first a little about me immediately before I joined Greenfield Online. I joined Engage Technologies as the general manager of the software division in 1998 and later became the division's president. The company's core products and services included Engage Knowledge, a database that contained more than 30 million anonymous consumer profiles, and AdManager, an online advertising management system that automated scheduling, targeting, and delivery of ads on Web sites and the reporting of online campaign results.

During my tenure at Engage, I learned that targeting advertising based on individuals' behaviors and interests was much more effective than simply running banner ads. This was in 1998, very early in the use of online advertising. At the time, Engage and DoubleClick were the only two advertising networks on the Internet. Both companies went public during the NASDAQ boom times and were racing to win the online advertising network market. It was an exciting time in 1998 but when it became evident that the stock market and business environment was about to take a huge turn for the worse, everything got weird. Well, maybe weird for that time. Actually, everything started to move back toward some level of rational business behavior.

"Back during the '90s dot-com era, there was a Boston-based company that was like an earlier version of what Google is today. It was an early adopter that pushed the limits of the Internet, which at the time was the new frontier. This company played a major part in laying down the foundation for what the Internet is today. The company was revolutionary. It had a powerful search engine, many different innovative products, Eric Schmidt's attention, and a venture arm. This company was CMGi in Andover, Massachusetts."[1]

CMGi's portfolio included companies like AltaVista, Engage, Lycos, GeoCities, Raging Bull, NaviSite, Furniture.com, MotherNature.com, MyWay.com, Snapfish, Yesmail, and many others.

Paul Schaut was CEO of Engage and my boss. He asked me to lead the software division of Engage. The "other" division was the advertising network. Our software was used by the advertising network division as their platform for online advertising and targeting. Soon after I started, Engage purchased two other Internet advertising companies from its corporate parent, CMGI, for stock valued at $2.5 billion. The companies, Adsmart and Flycast Communications, were to be fully integrated into Engage.

The move was seen as creating a stronger competitor to Internet advertising leader DoubleClick. Adsmart was an online advertising network for business-to-business and business-to-consumers markets. Flycast, based in San Francisco, provided direct response online advertising.

Engage's services included a profile-driven online marketing network, a database of more than 42 million consumer profiles, and an online advertising management system.

Paul Schaut was president and CEO of Engage, but George Garrick, chairman and CEO of Flycast and John Federman, president and CEO of Adsmart, joined Schaut in a new "office of the president" to oversee strategic operations at Engage.

"Online marketing is no longer about running a golf club banner ad on the golf section of a Web site and hoping your prospects click on it," Schaut said. "It's being accountable for identifying those prospects and turning them into repeat and loyal customers whenever they are on the Web."[2]

You can imagine with that type of attention to the mergers, the software division was left alone for me to lead. Meanwhile from January 2000, at the time of this merger/acquisition, the stock market bubble was leaking badly and ready to burst.

The New York Times ran an editorial on December 24, 2000: "The Dot Com Bubble Bursts." What a difference a year makes. The Nasdaq sank. Stock tips have been replaced with talk of recession. Many pioneering dot-coms are out of business or barely surviving. The Dow Jones Internet Index, made up of dot-com blue chips, is down more than 72 percent by March of 2001. Online retailers Priceline and eToys, former Wall Street darlings, have seen their stock prices fall more than 99 percent from their highs.[3]

Engage was navigating the merger during 2000 while attempting to do a secondary stock offering, but the market was shut down. Engage was on a path to run out of cash.

My phone rang and it is Ross Freeman, recruiter for Insight Partners. "Dean, how would you like to be a CEO?"

1

Always An Entrepreneur

C hallenging economic times bring out the entrepreneurial spirit in successful managers. My mother would say that I was an entrepreneur since I was a child. One winter, while living in Bethesda, Maryland, a snowstorm was predicted for the area. Bethesda doesn't get much snowfall each year and the weather forecasters generally were wrong about their predictions. This coming storm they were predicting over six inches. I was about ten years old at the time and saw this storm as an opportunity to make some money. I hit the street and started to make cold calls on the neighbors. I wanted to book up the demand before any competitors came around, so I pitched to do the shoveling job a day before the storm was predicted to arrive. I naturally targeted all of the neighbors who didn't have children or boys and wanted to be sure I covered a two-block radius of all potential customers. It was an easy sell. I offered to not take any money until the job was done, but to please give the job to me and be rest assured that I would be around when the snow begins to fade to get started. I would ask for payment upon completion. I think I booked 20 houses and started to count the money in my mind. I was going to be rich.

The winter of 1960 and 1961 may have been the heaviest snowfall in history for the Washington, D.C. area. In January more than 13 inches fell and in February it was more than 18 inches. Typically in a normal year less than 20 inches fall in the same area. The night of the first storm the snow seemed like it would never stop. I would go outside to our carport (we didn't have a garage) and look at the inches piling up and learn a valuable lesson about starting a business. Be certain you can deliver what you promise. By the end of the first house, with 19 more to go, I didn't think I could do it. I was exhausted after one. I knew quitting wasn't an option, my father instilled that into my brother and I since the first time we wanted to quit anything. He would say, "a Wiltse never quits." My first thought was to go ask my big brother Bob to come and help me. Of course he did, and by the third or fourth house we had to recruit my mother to come help us too. There we were, my mother, brother and I shoveling the entire neighborhood based on my sales ability or stupidity, probably a little of both. We finished, got paid, and that may be the last winter I was in the snow-shoveling business and only shoveled our own home every winter since.

I always worked different jobs growing up. From newspaper boy, to scooping ice cream at Baskin & Robbins, to camp counselor. My Dad worked for the government and my Mom was a high school teacher, so my brother and I had to earn extra spending money by working. Our sister came along when I was eight, further draining the family resources and driving our need for more money and finding jobs. Fortunately for us, our parents saved for our college, and our grandmother and my musician grandfather Fontanella saved money from his band leading as well as from owning dry cleaners and apartments to help my parents help us. Bob was a year older than me and he went off to Ithaca College after high school. I joined him there because they had an interest in my football ability and gave me a tryout.

The Ithaca College campus is situated on the side of a hill in upstate New York on the edge of the town of Ithaca. Cornell, a more famous college, was on an adjacent hill in town. The only place to buy food on campus was in the student union. Those of us in the upper quad area had about a half-mile walk down the hill to the dining room. After dinner was served the snack bar usually closed at 9 P.M. The winters in Ithaca were especially long, cold, snowy, and dark. It was also for the college (the 1970s) when no food or snacks were available on campus. Most students tried to solve the problem by getting refrigerators for their dorm room.

One cold fall, dark night on campus at Ithaca College, my roommate Marshall Grupp and I had a brainstorm: to sell sandwiches door to door at night when everyone is hungry and make some spending money. We were given permission by the school's admin department to do so, with the proviso that we'd get a food license and have health inspections from the town.

Our menu would include roast beef, cheese, ham and cheese, and tuna submarine sandwiches on white submarine bread rolls. My dorm had a small kitchen area where we proposed to make the sandwiches. Our strategy was to employ our friends (sales representatives) to sell the sandwiches by filling boxes with a variety of subs and for them to go from floor to floor in each dorm and yelling "subs." They would do this between the hours of 9 and 11 each weekday night. Marshall and I bought a meat slicer and found a local food distributor to sell us the bread, meats, cheeses and condiments, plastic wrap, and markers to write on the wrapped sandwich. We launched "Food For Thought" on Ithaca College campus with no fanfare. We even registered the name. We had permission to use the kitchen in our dorm. We started an assembly line in the kitchen and laid the bread out on the table. The table would hold about twenty sandwiches. We eventually added two more tables, as demand was immediate. One of us would walk down the line of bread and place the meat, then the other would place the cheese, someone would put on the condiments, then we would close, wrap in plastic, tape and label. We found file size cardboard boxes and placed about thirty premade subs in each of the boxes. We sent our friends out to assigned dorms carrying the boxes. They were paid a $1 commission on each sub sold. No salary. They had to sell to make money. We were smart enough not to pay by the hour, but by results achieved. Some of our friends were likely to eat some of the contents, so they had to come back with $150, which was thirty subs times a selling price of $5. Their commission was $1 per sub so they were happy to make $30 a box load. Our first night we sold one hundred and twenty subs in less than one hour. We had no inventory to make more and send them back out, so the next day we doubled the order for supplies. We made two hundred and forty subs the second night, which was eight boxes of thirty subs and they sold out in less than two hours. We didn't have a kitchen or refrigerator big enough to store extra items so we had to plan and execute to be profitable. We had no waste (one of our sellers bought six for himself). We were making so much money we became more focused on our new business than studying for class. Marshall and I were each profiting eighty dollars each per night, seven nights a week and our friends were each selling about fifty subs and making fifty dollars a night themselves. We took up skiing, bought all the equipment and purchased season passes, while playing on the football team.

After two years at Ithaca College I was bored with school. The Vietnam War was happening, so I transferred to avoid the draft. Staying out of the war was my motivation, not learning. My first full-time employment was straight commission sales for Lanier Business Products while I continued part time at school at night. They offered great training; at that time it was the Xerox Personal Selling Skills curriculum. Before the first day of the new job, everyone who joined the company had to memorize and be prepared to recite "The Sound Writing Story." This was a three- or four-page presentation of the history of Lanier, the company's vision, and how we typically helped customers. They would send all new sales people to the Basic Sales Training School in Atlanta for one week of intensive learning of their proven process for success. Upon arrival in Atlanta, each new employee would be required to recite verbatim to the group or to one of the instructors "The Sound Writing Story." We were told that if we failed to deliver it perfectly we would be sent home. As we traveled to Atlanta we naturally were studying and wondering at the same time if they would truly send us home if we didn't do well. We learned immediately they meant business. We also learned that they follow through and they inspect what they expect. Of the class of about twenty, two were sent home. The rest of us studied every night until late in the evening; it was all business.

I continued my career for eight years at Lanier. I learned many great business lessons. First, all compensation plans were totally aligned with the goals of your manager, branch manager, regional manager, and Vice President. As a new sales rep we were paid a commission on sales, and the more we sold the higher the rate. As managers we got an override commission on the commissions earned by the sales representatives reporting to the manager. As a branch manager we got a percentage of the profit generated by the branch. We would get a profit and loss statement monthly and learned quickly how to control expenses and increase sales.

The beginning of the microcomputer industry and Apple, in particular, was a trend I spotted and wanted to participate in. Due to my successful sales track record I was recruited to join one of the first Computerland franchises in the country located in Massachusetts. The owner was from Digital Equipment Company, and we rapidly grew to seven locations in New England. We expanded with B2B sales and commonly sold out of everything we could get our hands on from Apple and IBM at the time.

When you're faced with sudden new challenges, like the COVID-19 pandemic, you must think like you're starting your business all over again.

The first couple of days and weeks of any recession causes everyone to go into shock. I have lived through three as an adult and each time the impact of the recession begins to come to view, with everyone asking, "What does this mean?" This pandemic of 2020 shut down everything, literally everything: The travel industry, hospitality industry, and restaurants were shut down, and those that served those industries no longer had any business, such as airports, hotels, business offices, and restaurants, which were mandated to close.

The initial reaction of businesses when a recession starts is to cut all costs immediately; that usually begins with people. The managers of the business need to rally and come together to agree on a "new" strategy. The managers will need to involve the employees to be sure everyone understands what is happening and helps to reduce costs. Every expense item across every department must be scrutinized now that conditions are different. Assume no new sales will be made for the unforeseeable future. Identify any payables that you may owe and proactively reach out to see which payments can be delayed. You will be on the other side of calls like these, so don't be bashful. Call your landlord or bank to proactively work on a new payment plan. Look into marketing expenses and cancel what you can temporarily, including travel, until you get a better understanding of the recession. Your technology or IT infrastructure probably has expenses that can be reduced, so soliciting that team's assistance to dig in and help find savings will pay dividends.

Get back to your entrepreneurial roots and get everyone thinking about new needs that may arise from the recession. I will provide examples of sales strategies we implemented in past recessions, how we developed the ideas, and the ultimate positive impact that help save our business.

2

The Importance of Strong Investors

I have been the CEO of different companies in each of the last three recessions. During the early 2000s recession" (March of 2001 to November of 2001), I became Greenfield Online's CEO in March of 2001 until October of 2005. I joined Vovici in October of 2005 (it wasn't called Vovici at that time) and I left there in June 2009. That recession is now called "The Great Recession," which lasted December 2007 until June of 2009. I began consulting with RizePoint during October of 2019, accepted their offer to become CEO during January of 2020; I left there at the end of June 2020.

Without the investors at Greenfield Online we clearly wouldn't have existed. There were those that invested at the start of the company when it was a completely different vision. It seemed like a great idea at the time and lots of capital went into the company based on an idea that sounded like a good investment at that time. There was plenty of evidence that the marketing research industry could take advantage of the new Internet data capabilities, and Harris Interactive, a market research agency, was ahead in proving that value for investors could be created. But things did change with regard to global economics, and investors often had difficulty seeing an opportunity for change. At Greenfield Online we were fortunate to have sophisticated and experienced investors from Insight Venture Capital to support our new vision and to help navigate past the original investors that actually became obstacles in many cases.

My Greenfield Online opportunity happened because Peter Sobiloff, the Managing Director for Insight Venture Partners, believed in me. Of course the entire Board had to approve my coming on as CEO, but Peter was the one that met me on my initial interview and ultimately made the choice to hire me. I'm eternally grateful to him for making that happen. Peter was Chairman of the Board, and I reported to him my entire time as CEO. We worked closely together, and due to the way we navigated the business climate, the decisions we made, and the ultimate outcome, I consider Peter a friend for life.

Peter is a well-known executive in the software industry and regularly speaks on industry panels. He served as Chairman of Greenfield Online for six years, including three years as a public company. He was a member of the Board of Directors of Medidata Solutions for seven years. Other notable previous investments include Argus Software (acquired by Altus Group), DWL (acquired by IBM), Enigma (acquired by PTC), GETPAID (acquired by Sunguard), Netsmart Technologies (acquired by Genstar Financial), iMany (IPO), Kinnser Software (acquired by Mediware), Nistevo (acquired by Sterling Software), Overdrive (acquired by Rakuten), Paisley (acquired by Thomson Reuters), PerTrac (acquired by eVestment), Planview (sold majority to Thoma Bravo), Primavera (acquired by Oracle), Rockport Trade Systems (acquired by QRS Corp), and Shunra (sold to Hewlett-Packard).

Peter currently serves on the Board of Directors at Achieve3000, DrillingInfo, Duco, Fenergo, Filmtrack, Kony Solutions, NYMBUS, Planview, Mediaspectrum, and Workforce Software.

Peter is the type of man everyone simply likes. He is a great listener, never speaks about himself, and is dedicated to helping the people around him in every way. I was never afraid to discuss any issue with Peter, regardless of the complexity or potential ramifications. I knew I would get a well-thought-out opinion on any issue based on his experience. If he wasn't comfortable with commenting he would usually say, "This is a question for Jeff." Jeff was Jeff Horing, Peter's partner at Insight and also on the Board at Greenfield Online. I also learned to respect Jeff's thoughts and opinions, for Jeff was a very strategic thinker and extremely brilliant.

Jeff Horing, who worked at Warburg Pincus and Goldman Sachs prior to founding Insight Venture Partners (he was a co-founder and has been Managing Director at Insight since 1995), was instrumental to the strategy decisions we made. We wouldn't have accomplished our success without his support and contributions. Under his leadership, Insight has become a premier venture capital and private equity firm with more than $20 billion of assets under management. Jeff's areas of focus include data, analytics, mobile, infrastructure, and SaaS in Europe, North America, and Israel. Jeff has invested in more than 30 companies, notably Alteryx, AirWatch (acquired by VMware), Shutterstock, TeamViewer (acquired by Permira), WIX, and Greenfield Online (later acquired by Microsoft).

The entire Insight team was amazing to work with. Their model is to help the management teams of their portfolio companies with advice, introductions, and experience. Deven Parekh is a Managing Director at Insight Venture Partners and joined the firm in 2000. Bob Bies our CFO, worked more with Deven at Insight than he did with other investors.

Jeff Lieberman has been at Insight since its earliest days and has been an active investor in both SaaS software and consumer Internet companies. Jeff is focused on partnering with great entrepreneurs across the globe and helping them scale their businesses. He has led or co-led nearly fifty deals across four continents since joining Insight in 1998.

Nikitas Koutoupes is now a Managing Director at Insight Venture Partners, and joined the firm in 2001 just after I joined Greenfield

Online. He became a part of our operating team. He was just getting started at Insight about the same time I was getting started at Greenfield. He spent many days working with our operational teams and participated in many of our management team discussions. Prior to Insight, Nikitas co-founded and was the Chief Financial Officer of CTSpace, a software company that became part of Insight's portfolio and was subsequently acquired by the Sword Group. He was previously with McKinsey & Company, where he worked on strategy, turnaround, M&A, and corporate finance engagements. He also contributed to a major research initiative entitled "The War For Talent." Nikitas co-authored a chapter titled "Customer Lifetime Value: Methodology and Applications for Operating Partners," in *The Operating Partner in Private Equity*, published by Private Equity International. Nikitas received an MBA from Harvard Business School, where he was a Baker Scholar. He earned a BA from Princeton University's Woodrow Wilson School of Public and International Affairs, graduating summa cum laude. He is an example of the quality people that were available to us as a management team.

Nikitas has had continual success over the years. He focuses on investments in education technology and sales and marketing automation, and is one of the firm's experts in recurring revenue business models. He currently works with Academic Partnerships, Campaign Monitor, CarTrawler, Conga, CloudCraze, Ensighten, Illuminate Education, KDS, Nearpod, SpaceTime Games, and Virgin Pulse. Nikitas's prior investments at Insight include Capella University Exact Target (acquired by Salesforce); eVestment (acquired by Nasdaq); Football Fanatics (acquired by GSI Commerce, then eBay); Frontline (acquired by Thoma Bravo); Greenfield Online (acquired by Microsoft); Platespin (acquired by Novell); and Realink (acquired by Zaio Corp). He was named to the AlwaysOn Venture Capital 100. For the first decade of his tenure at Insight, Nikitas co-managed Insight Onsite, the firm's team of dedicated operations and strategy experts.[4]

Scott Maxwell has been a Venture Capitalist since 2000, first as a senior Managing Director at Insight Venture Partners and then as the founder of OpenView. At OpenView, and previously at Insight, he worked to develop and communicate the vision that an institutionalized venture capital firm can—and should—offer beyond the capital that it invests. Scott has spent over a decade iterating on that approach, which includes the development of the investment focus and team, OpenView Labs team, and content sites for executives. I refer to their sites often and share the information with those I feel need to learn more about the SaaS business model, which has become predictable as more and more software companies have adopted offering software applications in the cloud. An annual survey of SaaS company executives was also conducted and the results were made available for comparison. Scott's vision about venture capital firms offering meaningful value is what OpenView is all about. For me, Insight is truly different from the other venture firms I have worked with. I haven't directly worked with OpenView but have worked with Scott before he started OpenView. I can assume they are similar in their approach to their portfolio companies and executives.

Larry Handen was a Managing Director at UBS and on our Board of Directors and eventually went to work with Insight. We developed a great working relationship and I learned to fully respect his intelligence and deep understanding of business and finances. Larry and I were actually co-members of the company's "acquisition committee" and together with Bob Bies made the recommendation to the Board to acquire Ciao (Ciao was ultimately the reason Microsoft purchased Greenfield Online). During his career, Larry has been involved as a principal investor in more than 175 M&A and equity financing transactions, and served on the Board of Directors of more than 40 companies throughout the world. Additionally, he has advised more than 100 other companies in various capacities.

Some of Larry's former portfolio companies include Primavera (acquired by Oracle), Greenfield Online (acquired by Microsoft), Netsmart (acquired by Genstar Financial), Guardant (acquired by VeriSign), DivX (acquired by Rovi), Commvault, SecureInfo (acquired by Kratos Defence), Digital Harbor (acquired by Norkom Technologies), Dynamicsoft (acquired by Cisco), 3P Learning, (Lytx acquired by GTCR), MV Sistemas, Overdrive, Photobox (acquired by Elctra), Planview (acquired by Thoma Bravo), Informatica, Tritech (acquired by Bain), Compassus, Achieve, Laureate, Healthsun (acquired by Anthem) Privalia (acquired by Vente-Privee), and Trilogy.

Prior to Macquarie, where Larry is now, Larry was a Managing Director at Insight Venture Partners. Prior to Insight, Mr. Handen was a General Partner at UBS Capital where he led the firm's Software, Internet & Services Group. Previously, he was a Partner with PricewaterhouseCoopers Consulting. While at PwC, Larry led a practice specializing in corporate-wide growth and recovery solutions for companies in the technology, information, communications, and entertainment industries.

You can see that I was surrounded by capable, experienced, and very smart people. After my success at Greenfield Online I was fortunate to work with other investment firms at other companies. There is a huge difference due to the people. All of the Insight team was extremely valuable.

Insight Venture Partners owned a majority of the stock of Greenfield Online. I was fortunate to have this world-class team as my support mechanism throughout the ups and downs, and we had both. During 2001 we had to determine the strategy to save the business. Once we agreed on the strategy, we needed to execute and deliver results. Once we delivered strong results we had to consider options to fund the business, IPO, sell, raise additional capital, and borrow from banks. After we completed the IPO we needed to determine our strategy to grow globally, to determine the best acquisitions, negotiate the purchase, and integrate the companies with us. Having strong investors is essential to success. Over the last twenty years as CEO of other opportunities, I learned to value the people and value of investors like Insight Venture Partners, Chris Pacitti, David Lack, and Rajeev Batra at the Mayfield Fund.

3

Discovering Greenfield Online

The Board of Directors at Greenfield Online had made a decision to make a change at the top: the CEO. They also needed to try to save the company during an extremely challenging business climate (January 2001). The current CEO had been leading the vision that Greenfield Online was running as the company made its way toward an IPO as a marketing research company. Greenfield's difference from similar firms—the business model was largely the same as TNS or NFO and other large marketing research organizations—was that they were going to change the way the world conducted research projects: by collecting data from the Internet instead of using telephone or face-to-face surveys. Their team of research experts was competing with marketing research firms that had been in business for decades. The difference was they collected their survey data online. They offered the same services as traditional marketing research firms, just a different method of collecting survey data.

Hiring was done in anticipation of growing the company rapidly after the planned IPO for 1999 or 2000. Harris Interactive was a direct competitor that had recently gone public with a similar business proposition. The Harris Poll had been conducted by doing telephone research, and in 2000 they were one of the first to have an online survey panel.

Someone new needed to come in to lead the investors and the employees in a dramatically different direction. No one knew what that meant yet, but they did know that costs needed to be cut dramatically.

I met with Peter Sobiloff from Insight Venture Partners in a hotel in Wilton, Connecticut (I was living in Andover, Massachusetts at the time). Peter was Chairman of the Board and Managing Partner with Insight Venture Partners, the largest shareholder in Greenfield Online. During our meeting he described how the company was losing cash by thousands of dollars each month, and the remaining cash from a recent capital raise would be gone in months if expenses were not cut immediately. Peter was very interested in the "custom" marketing research business due to the low margin and services business model. Even though the research data was being collected via a new methodology—online versus telephone—the company was still doing analysis and recommendations based on the data. Also, the people doing that analysis were expensive and the number of projects being sold wasn't growing. In fact, due to the business climate new projects were not materializing. The investors were looking for someone to help "right size" the business so that the expenses were not more than the business being sold and delivered.

I learned about a software product under development at Greenfield Online called QuickTake. No revenue had been generated by QuickTake, but it was a survey software solution that had promise. Software business models are typically higher margin than services businesses, and QuickTake made it easy to build a survey and collect answers from the Greenfield Online panel or respondents rapidly and at a low cost.

Fieldsource was another product being sold. It was the offering of access to the Greenfield Online panel database to other custom marketing research firms. The "custom research" people didn't sell it. Their business proposition was their analysis of the data and the design of the survey. The design of a survey does require experts so that the person responding is not led in any specific or a biased direction. Fieldsource would offer to invite people from the Greenfield Online panel to discuss other online surveys that would be programmed and hosted by other research firms, which would do the analysis of the survey results. I would come to find out immediately, literally within hours of joining the company, about the internal conflict between the "custom" team and the Fieldsource team at the company.

My meeting with Peter went well, so he scheduled me to meet with Jeff Horing, Managing Partner at Insight Venture Partners; Bob Bies, CFO at GOL; Jonathan Flatow, VP Corp Council; and Joel Meznick, another board member.

The meetings that Bob and Jonathan held were very interesting. Bob was the CFO and Jonathan the legal counsel. Both had been with the company for several years and desperately wanted it to succeed because the company was preparing for an IPO just before the dotcom bubble burst and the time and effort necessary to find bankers as well as preparing the initial offering document was extremely demanding of them. I can see they were frustrated. Both of them helped the company every step of the way after my arrival: through our IPO, our secondary offering, and the acquisitions of Opinion Survey, Rapidata, goZing, and Ciao! After I left, Bob and Jonathan were at the company through the acquisition by Microsoft.

When I joined, it was *the* day the company was moving their headquarters to a brand new space next door to where we interviewed. They gave me a quick tour during our interview and I could see they were a little embarrassed about the investment being made considering the company's condition. It was a beautiful space with a modern reception area and open kitchen with TV screens. The kitchen had bar stools, bar and nice open area for employee gatherings and meetings. My office had electronic doors on each end with garage door type of controls. I could sit in my desk chair and click a button for my office door to open and close. There was a door at each end of my office that operated with a click of a button. At one end was a beautiful conference room with a drop down screen, surround sound and remote control for drapes, lighting and screens. The other end opened to the hall and a third sliding door connected to a small office where my secretary would sit. I never had a secretary or electronic doors before. I was always embarrassed about the office I inherited. First impressions are always important and my style has never been flamboyant. The office was nice for employees, but my space was over the top.

The meeting with Joel Meznik, another board member, was brief and in the Starbucks below the new office. I had been told that Joel was the one who recommended the current CEO to the board and was a big fan of his. I could tell Joel wasn't comfortable. I felt he only met with me because the largest shareholder told him he had to. I don't know that was true, but Joel and I never bonded. He was an original investor and stayed on the board until Greenfield sold to Microsoft in 2008.

The offer to be the CEO came. I would be allowed to commute from my Boston home as long as I wanted and housing would be provided for me next to the office: a nice new townhouse across the parking lot from the office. Compensation was fair and I truly believed I could have a positive impact on the business. I had no custom marketing research experience, but we had plenty of that experience with people at the company. The board asked that I meet with Bob and Jonathan a few weeks prior to being announced to the company employees to plan my first days and to execute a strategy to reduce costs immediately. The plan would not only entail a headcount reduction but a plan to reduce costs everywhere we could. I accepted the position as CEO to start in March of 2001.

The former CEO would never move into his new office because the execution of our plan to reduce costs started on the day before the move was to take place.

The NASDAQ Composite March 2001, my start date at Greenfield Online was 2,631.57.

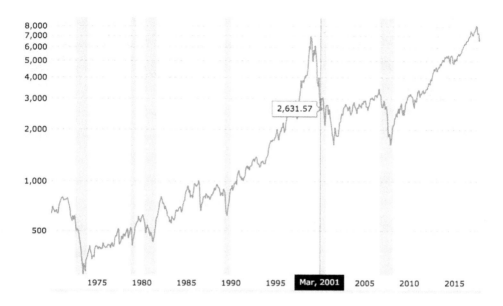

While the business climate continued to deteriorate in 2001, we set on a path to experience significant growth in our revenues related to Internet survey solutions since 2000. Starting with a base annual revenue of $2.1 million in 2000, our Internet survey solutions revenues grew to $25.9 million for the year ended December 31, 2003.[5] Here is how we did it.

4

Go To Market Strategy

B ob Bies was our CFO at Greenfield Online. I didn't hire Bob but he was essential to our success. In fact, I don't believe we would have accomplished what we did if it were not for Bob. I never spent much time before Greenfield Online with people who achieved a 4.0 grade point average in college and graduate school, but Bob did. He majored in Biochemistry at Long Island University, CW Post for his BS and MBA at Hofstra. He got his CPA and went to work for Deloitte. He brought that same work ethic that got him those 4.0 grade point averages to Greenfield. I will take credit for being a good listener and collaborator.

We had a great management team that I cannot take credit for hiring. I can take credit for managing the team to achieve great things. We created an environment to reward winning and eliminating obstacles. I learned early on in my career that "attitude is everything" and have always worked toward uniting the vision and defining clear goals and methods to achieve them.

I was commuting from Boston and living in a hotel until I found an apartment. Bob and his family were extremely generous to me. We had many dinners together at their home at the end of long days. Many fun nights, but also many nights discussing our business challenges.

We established the plan to make the CEO change and to reduce expenses. The company had done two reductions in force (RIFs) during the previous six months to my joining. Our goal was to make this RIF the last so we could attempt to put everyone's mind at ease and focus on fixing our business. We didn't want me to walk in and let people go, so Bob, Jonathan, and Peter were to deliver the news to those being terminated. The plan was for Peter Sobiloff to call the then current CEO and ask him to meet Peter in NYC at the Insight offices. There Peter would thank him and provide the necessary termination information. Bob and Jonathan were to schedule group meetings simultaneously at 9 A.M. on Monday, the same time Peter was meeting with the CEO. The idea of the group meetings was to lessen the impact so everyone could see it wasn't only affecting them. Individual meetings were scheduled after the group meetings to answer specific questions. I was to stay away from the office while the RIF was happening. People were asked to leave within the hour and take their belongings with them.

All went according to plan. These were difficult situations for everyone. Obviously, those who were terminated were the most who affected, but those delivering the news and those who remained had to deal with and accept the changes. Those who remained not only had the anxiety of seeing their coworkers terminated, but they also needed to cover their work and then worry if another RIF is going to happen.

Bob called me around 10:30 A.M. as did Peter. All terminations were handled professionally and it was expected everyone would be out of the headquarters by 11 A.M. There was a group located out of the office that was called as a group and also terminated via telephone conference during this time frame.

I arrived around 11 A.M. and we conducted a companywide meeting in the kitchen and dialed in the remote people to announce me to the company. Peter Sobiloff and Joel Mesnick, two members of the board, also attended. They did their best to explain to everyone why the actions had to happen and to announce their appreciation to everyone and their regrets for the hardship and predicament the company was in and also the country. This type of action was happening everywhere.

On March 10, 2000, the NASDAQ traded at 5,048.62. The all-time high was in September of 2000, at 6969. In 1999, 65.9 percent of the Nasdaq were technology stocks, such as Cisco, Oracle, and Qualcomm. Telecom made up Another 15.2 percent. The remaining stock portions consisted of 5 percent consumer, 6.2 percent health-care, 4 percent financials, and 3.7 percent of other types.

Year	Unemployment Rate (December)	GDP Growth	Inflation (December Year-over-Year)
1998	4.4%	4.5%	1.6%
1999	4.0%	4.8%	2.7%
2000	3.9%	4.1%	3.4%
2001	5.7%	1.0%	1.6%
2002	6.0%	1.7%	2.4%
2003	5.7%	2.9%	1.9%
2004	5.4%	3.8%	3.3%
2005	4.9%	3.5%	3.4%

Unemployment grew to one of its highest rates since 1993 at 5.7% in 2001 and 6% in 2002. It stayed at 5.7% in 2003.

NASDAQ was down to 2631 in March 2001. It still had a way to go down to reach its low in September of 2002, 1631.

I was introduced as the new CEO. People were visibly upset. I read the faces and remember I was surprised at the wide range of emotions on people's faces: mostly sadness and anger along with a few smiles.

Mara Shelby hit me with the toughest questions. Mara was a very experienced marketing researcher (as I write these words she's a VP at Harris Interactive). Soon after I started we promoted Mara to Chief Research Officer at Greenfield. She held the respect of everyone and managed the largest accounts generating research revenues for the company. She knew marketing research. I did not. Steve Cook, now Executive Vice President at Target Research Group, pioneered online research at Greenfield and was no longer with the company. I learned how respected he was by everyone. He held the position of Senior Vice President of Sales at Greenfield prior to me joining. I eventually met Steve a few years later. He and Mara are just two examples of the great people at Greenfield Online who believed the company would become the most innovative custom marketing research firm using the Internet for data collection.

During my first several hours at the company I tried to meet as many people individually as possible. My goal was to understand the company and try to quickly determine a strategy to save it. Literally within hours of meeting with at least a dozen people I was shocked how everyone was more focused inwardly on internal tensions versus being focused on selling the services the company offered. The people there had pretty much figured out that the custom marketing research business and the Fieldsource business were conflicting and sent a conflicting message to prospects of both products. Everyone sensed the tension and spoke about it in almost every meeting with me.

During my first few days a prospective client company visit had been scheduled with the CEO of Market Facts, a large custom marketing research firm based in Chicago. The CEO and several people from the company traveled to Wilton for the meeting. There they learned the Greenfield Online CEO they thought they were coming to see had been replaced by me. Market Facts was coming because the salesperson for the Fieldsource products convinced them to use the Greenfield Online survey panelist as their data source. Fieldsource clients that have their own survey programming capabilities, like Market Facts, which have limited or no access to survey respondents, can purchase controlled access to the Greenfield Online panel. Custom marketing research firms typically sell their expertise to brands. That expertise—designing surveys, analyzing the survey data results, and making recommendations to the brands—is what custom marketing researchers do to make money. They need people to answer surveys. During that time, 2001, the most prevalent way to get people to answer surveys was to call them on the telephone or have an interviewer stop people in the mall. Online surveys were just getting started.

The Market Facts CEO spelled things out very clearly. He told me that the entire marketing research industry at that time would spend 60% of their revenues on collecting data for their clients' brands. They would pay companies that had a staff of trained survey interviewers to dial the phone and get people to answer their surveys. They would design surveys with their expertise, use telephone calls and face-to-face meetings with interviewers to get answers to questions in their surveys. The wording of the questions as well as the order the answer choices were asked were all very important for collecting meaningful data. The research firms would then analyze the answers and make recommendations to the brands. That is how they made money. The people doing the survey design and analysis had to be well trained and experienced. After all *big* decisions would be made based on the results. A good example was the survey Greenfield Online had done for Frito about an idea to color tortilla chips purple. At the time there was no such thing as a purple chip. As a result of the research and recommendations that a purple chip would be successful, Frito invested huge amounts and launched the new product.

Most of the employees at Greenfield Online worked in the "Custom Research" division. They actually competed with all custom marketing research firms like Market Facts. The CEO of Market Facts told me to "get out of the custom research business and just sell us access to your online survey panel. We will pay for every survey that is completed. Leave it to us to sell the research project to the brand, design the surveys, and analyze the results. Just invite your panelist to come to our surveys online."

The core asset that had been built with the millions of dollars invested in Greenfield Online was the survey panel. We actively managed the Greenfield Online panel, a 100% Internet-based panel of approximately 1.7 million individuals who participated in our surveys. Our panelists represent households consisting of an estimated 4.7 million people, allowing us to compile diverse, demographically representative survey data. We tried to maintain 70 different attributes about the individuals. Getting survey results was faster, better, and cheaper on the Internet versus other methodologies, like telephone or face-to-face interviews. The research industry hadn't yet validated or approved the Internet as a valid method for gathering research. The concern in the late 1990s and early 2000s was that the Internet was only used by a more affluent demographic and would only be valid for types of research that was only interested in them. There was also the problem that research firms become accustomed to their practices and methods and using a new method was unfamiliar and potentially dangerous to the analysis conclusions.

He was the first one to make this suggestion to me, to get out of the custom research business—and this was within my first three days at the company! Now I had a large research company CEO telling me our online panel was very valuable to his company and employees inside the company were battling for control. I was shocked by how much energy custom research employees were wasting focused on our Fieldsource offering. Our custom researchers wanted us to stop selling access to other researchers and our Fieldsource sales person was getting traction selling our panel to our custom research division's competitors.

One of my first days I needed to travel into NYC to meet with our largest investor. I had a car service pick me up at the office to bring me into the city. I got in the car and the driver said to me "I thought I might be waiting here for hours." I said, "Why would you think that?" He responded "There was a lady who traveled from California fairly regularly to your office. She would have drivers wait all day for her, sometimes eight to ten hours just sitting in the car in the parking lot. We would then drive her to a restaurant or to her nearby hotel. The bill was sometimes over one thousand dollars just to sit and wait." You can imagine my surprise at hearing this. I asked for the name. I quickly determined that she was on the list of people that were terminated. It turns out this same individual would have a bouquet of flowers sent to herself each week to her desk at company expense. Those were the bubble days, I guess.

5

The Right Strategy

Looking back I am amazed at our execution and speed to making critical decisions at each of the companies, but especially Greenfield Online. This is essential in any down economy. Survival is a strong motivator. The cash raised by the company as bridge financing was going to run out a few months after I started. We were going to need to ask for more but obviously needed a reason for investors to believe we could survive and not just lose more of their money. We hadn't figured out a plan yet; I had only been with the company a few weeks but the investors needed to be informed of the impending need for cash.

We had a special Board of Directors call set up and I traveled into NYC. Bob Bies, our CFO, and Jonathan Flatow, our corporate counsel and secretary, stayed at the office on the telephone. The timing of this meeting was approximately April or May of 2001 (I started March of 2001). After Bob took the board through the numbers, the reductions we made, and our current estimated burn rate, we faced many questions. One question that I will never forget wasn't made by Insight but another board member. He asked, "Can we ask all the employees to forgo taking their pay for a few months?" As a first time CEO, I never imagined that question could be asked. I didn't respond immediately, I was shocked but also not sure if he was serious. After a few moments of silence I said, "I am sorry I didn't join this company to ask people such a thing." He persisted to describe his feelings about the losses in the company's past, the investment made to date, and that he didn't have an appetite to put more money in. I could certainly understand that sentiment based on what I had learned about the business in my short tenure, but didn't think that I could be making such a request of people we are asking every day to work hard to save the business—especially when there was no equity value in their stock options. It did drive home to me the dire situation the company and all employees could face in just a few weeks.

His tone of voice and facial expressions were that of a desperate man. My mind was racing and I wasn't sure how to react or what to say. After a few more minutes of the conversation going down the path of considering whether to ask employees to work for free or not, I stood up and said "I didn't sign up for this. I am happy to lead this company back to being cash flow positive but we are going to need a few million to give us more time. We can come back to the board with a solid plan in a few more weeks, but we will need a little more time." I walked out.

As I made it down the elevator and stepped out on 5th Avenue, I just started walking. I was now possibly unemployed during a horrible recession and walked out of my first CEO opportunity. What will I tell my family? What will happen to all the employees and the company? Then my phone rang, it was Jonathan. He said "Nice work. They agreed to give us the money. Go back."

With the current COVID-19 pandemic I found myself in a similar situation at another company. It seems when investors are tired and have been in an investment for several years they can be detrimental to making good decisions. Investors' past frustrations with the company makes them fear that it will be a never-ending saga of deeper losses. Try to align yourself and your business with investors who have experience in other companies with a similar business model and those who have navigated difficult economic times in their past investments. I was fortunate at Greenfield Online with Insight Venture Partners. They had confidence and the staying power with additional funding capability. So much in fact, they designed a "cram down round" which meant that any of the past investors who chose not to invest in the final $2 million to be raised for Greenfield Online would lose the value of all their equity invested from past funding rounds. This allowed Insight to capture more ownership and to give management and employees an option pool to share in future success. This is positive motivation for employees, the exact opposite of what tired investors were suggesting. Cut employee pay? Or give them an ownership stake at reasonable value to be motivated to achieve great results during very challenging economic times. Which would you pick? It seems like an obvious choice. Unfortunately for many companies their investors are people with money who lack the experience of running a company. As a consequence, they can kill your business or create serious problems as a result.

It was the sense of urgency created at that meeting that drove Bob, Jonathan, and me to quickly make tough choices. We knew we needed others at the company to give us their thoughts and ideas on how we can grow, reduce expenses, and save the company. The next several weeks and months brought Hugh Davis, co-founder of Greenfield Online, and Keith Price, sales representative for Fieldsource, to the management team made up of Bob, Jonathan, and myself.

Hugh's story was that when Andy Greenfield came up with the idea for the company, Hugh was an intern. Andy had a research company needing some research to be conducted for a client and was looking for a young demographic—college students—to answer some survey questions. Andy asked Hugh to pull together a focus group and offer to hire an interviewer, pay $100 per respondent to answer, and get the survey results. Within a few hours, Hugh walked back into Andy's office and told him the survey was done and that he didn't need any money to pay any expenses. "How did you do that?" Andy asked Hugh. "I sent the survey in my email to my friends and asked them to forward it around and send their answers back to me." That was the start of using the Internet for collecting survey responses for marketing research. Hugh was about 18 years old when he started and when I arrived he was in his twenties.

Hugh's office was next to mine. Everyone was going in and out of his office constantly. I could overhear the conversations, which was a great education for me. Hugh managed the GOL panel of 1.7 million and the team of people who programmed the surveys. He also emailed invitations to people based on their profile to answer the survey questions. That was how we got paid. The custom research team also charged for their expertise of designing the survey questions and analyzing the results. Those people were highly paid experts and the profit margins on their projects were low. Our costs included the expense of the brainpower for custom projects. The Fieldsource projects didn't require any analysis or design expertise. They did need to become experts in managing the panel, the data, and routing people to surveys online. Margins were very high for our Fieldsource projects. Hugh led the teams that recruited more people to our panel, programmed surveys for our custom research team, and invited panelists to follow links in our emails to surveys hosted by other marketing research firms.

In order to grow our business, regardless of whether the projects were sold by the custom research group or by the Fieldsource team, we needed more and more people to join our panel and take surveys. We used a number of methods back in those days to attract people to join our online survey panel. Rewards and contests were generally the message. One of our best methods was a link on the home page of MSN.com. In 2001 MSN was one of the most trafficked websites. This logo was used from 2000 to 2009, you probably remember it or have seen it:

In 1998, the largely underutilized MSN.com domain name was combined with Microsoft Internet Start and reinvented as both a Web portal and as the brand for a family of sites produced inside Microsoft's Interactive Media Group. The new website put MSN in direct competition with sites such as Yahoo!, Excite, and Go Network.

Because the new format opened up MSNs content to the world for free, the Internet service provider and subscription service was renamed MSN Internet Access at that time.

MSN launched a search portal called MSN Search, using search results from Inktomi. After many changes to the backend search engine, MSN would start developing in-house search technology in 2005 and later change its name to Bing in June 2009.

MSN.com became the successor to the default Internet Explorer start page, as all of the previous "Microsoft Internet Start" website was merged with MSN.com. Some of the original websites that Microsoft launched during that era remain active in some form today. Microsoft Investor, a business news and investments service that was once produced in conjunction with CNBC, is now MSN Money; CarPoint, an automobile comparison and shopping service, is now MSN Autos; and the Internet Gaming Zone, a website offering online casual games, is now MSN Games. Other websites since divested by Microsoft include the travel website Expedia, the online magazine *Slate*, and the local event and city search website, Sidewalk.com.

In the late 1990s, Microsoft collaborated with many other service providers as well as other Microsoft departments to expand the range of MSN's services. Some examples include MSN adCenter, MSN Shopping (affiliated with eBay, PriceGrabber, and Shopping.com), and the Encarta encyclopedia with various levels of access to information. Since then, MSN.com has remained a popular destination, launching many new services and content sites. MSN's Hotmail and Messenger services were promoted from the MSN.com portal, which provided a central place for all of MSN's content. MSN Search (now Bing), a dedicated search engine, launched in 1999. The single sign-in service for Microsoft's online services, Microsoft Passport (now Microsoft account), also launched across all MSN services in 1999. The MSN.com portal and related group of services under the MSN umbrella remained largely the same in the early 2000s. The sports section of the MSN portal was ESPN.com from 2001 to 2004.[6]

One of our brilliant moves in 2001 was to enter into a deal with MSN.com that didn't cost us a penny. We entered into an agreement that would allow us to intercept their traffic by putting a link on their homepage. The link would say something like "Get Rewards" or "Win Cash." Things that sound interesting these days were new to people surfing the Web in 2001. We were the first online survey panel. When someone clicked on our link they were taken to a landing page where they were encouraged to join our survey panel. Those that opted in to join were designated in our panel as coming from MSN. The agreement stated we would pay MSN.com something every time we were paid by one of our clients for getting someone that joined our panel from MSN to complete a survey. This was brilliant in several ways. Our cost of goods was the cost we would incur to recruit people to join our survey panel. It usually costs money to get links on a website such as MSN. We eliminated our immediate costs for adding new survey panelists by making the cost incremental to when we would get paid for someone completing a survey. The other brilliant move was that we only used the MSN people in our panel when we *really* needed to use them. If we had a survey that we had trouble completing from our day-to-day panel, that was when we would use the MSN panel that we built.

We introduced this new survey methodology as "The River" in 2001. The "MSN River" was a continual flow of new people joining our survey panel every day. Not only did our panel of 1.7 million households differentiate us in the market, but adding "The River" with MSN differentiated us and helped us be known as the leader in online marketing research methods. As of May 2005, MSN.com was the second most visited portal website in the United States with a share of 23.2 percent, behind Yahoo!, which held a majority. I left the company in October of 2005 when the relationship with MSN.com was still active. Three years later Microsoft purchased Greenfield Online. Their motivation had nothing to do with our survey business.

Now that we had a clear source for continued survey takers I came to the decision to exit the custom marketing research business and focus on Fieldsource. Selling the survey responses of our panel members to other marketing research firms was a very high-margin business. It also served a demand that we were creating in the research industry for more online survey research. By getting out of the custom business we would no longer be a competitor to other research firms and we could supply them with online survey panelists to take their surveys. We would reduce our costs by no longer needing highly paid researchers to work on the survey projects. The customers of our Fieldsource offering would do the design of the survey and analyze the results. We just needed to offer the ability to program their surveys online and invite our panelist to take them.

We also developed a brilliant sales strategy to convince marketing research firms to use online panelists versus the way they were familiar for years. Many research companies had even developed telephone call centers where interviewers would make hundreds of telephone calls each day to get people to answer surveys on the telephone. They knew that they would need to make hundreds if not thousands of telephone calls to get people to take the time to answer and then they needed to be sure they had "representative data." This means the general population makeup needed to be represented in the survey results. A representative sample is one that accurately represents, reflects, or "is like" your population. A representative sample should be an unbiased reflection of what the population is like. There are many ways to evaluate representativeness: gender, age, socioeconomic status, profession, education, chronic illness, even personality or pet ownership. It all depends on how detailed you want to get, the scope of your study, and what information about your population is available. One of the advantages of an online survey panel was that we could develop a record of how they answered questions in the past, which means that we didn't have to always ask again and again.

The reason for our existence as a company was that we had developed a faster, better, cheaper way of collecting survey data. Now we had to convince the research firms and the brands that our data was just as good as the telephone data or the face-to-face data they had been collecting for years.

We decided to offer a few large research firms the opportunity to give us their most recent survey project that they had fielded on the telephone and not share the results with us. We would perform the exact same survey online and deliver the results in 24 hours, for free, so they could see if it was the same. If the results were the same, they would agree to use us and we would charge them one-half of what they paid the telephone call center. We got their attention. You see, for marketing research firms, almost 50% of their cost of doing business was to collect survey responses for their clients. Paying telephone call centers took weeks to months to get the right number of responses, and they were paying humans to do each and every survey with someone who would agree to answer. An automated telephone survey is a systematic collection of data from demography[7] by making calls automatically to the preset list of respondents at the aim of collecting information and gain feedback via the telephone. Automated surveys are used for customer research purposes by call centers for customer relationship management and performance management purposes. They are also used for political polling, market research, and job satisfaction surveying. An automated phone survey applies the interactive voice response system is any telephone system that interacts with callers without input from a human other than the caller. More specifically, interactive voice response, or IVR, is the technology that automates telephone contact between humans and machines. OK, this sounds a little more cost effective, but imagine how you react when you get one of these calls. People hate it. The costs for doing this method of research was getting more costly and people were not answering. Along came Greenfield Online.

We got several research firms to take us up on our offer to do a comparison survey using a recent telephone survey. We did it quickly, within hours, got the results we needed, and delivered them back. The response was astounding. The results compared were weeks faster and our planned cost would be one-half the price.

Everyone can relate to how it felt to being interrupted at home for an unexpected telephone call. These days most of us don't have landlines; we only have our cell phones. Back in 2001 fewer than one or two percent didn't have telephones in their home.

In May of 2017 the data was released. It showed that most U.S. homes no longer use landline phone service and instead rely on cell phones to stay connected. The finding was by the U.S. Health Department, which said that 50.8 percent of American households were now wireless only when it came to phone service. Of the remaining chunk of households, 39.4 percent had both a wireless phone and a landline. Only 6.5 percent of homes are landline only, while 3.2 percent remain phone-free.

The figures, based on a telephone poll of nearly 20,000 households, show just how quickly Americans have abandoned landlines. Just 10 years ago, only about 15 percent of households were wireless only. But the number has risen sharply as smartphones became more prominent, and it looks like the wireless-only homes are bound to keep growing.[8]

Our financial performance in the Fieldsource side of the business was terrific. We had validated the marketing research firms would buy our "online sample." We had proven the data was similar to familiar methods. We even went the extra step to hire a university professor to validate that the online survey sample was similar to reaching people by telephone.

We quickly made the decision to exit the custom research business and focus on selling access to our panel to marketing research firms. Next step: get Board approval. Our recommendation was to sell the custom research business to an existing research firm and secure a contract from the acquirer of that business to supply them with their survey response needs.

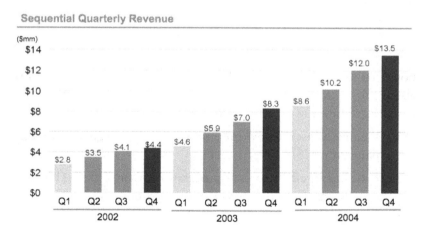

Sequential Quarterly Revenue

Another Positive Force

The Federal Trade Commission (FTC) amended the Telemarketing Sales Rule (TSR) to give consumers a choice about whether they want to receive most telemarketing calls. The Bureau of Labor Statistics estimated there were nearly a quarter of a million people in the U.S. employed as telemarketers. With each one making dozens or hundreds of calls a day, it's no wonder your phone was ringing off the hook. That doesn't even include the thousands of automated robo callers and scammers out there who might drop you a line as well. Telemarketing has been an annoyance for decades, which is why it's so surprising that the National Do Not Call Registry didn't come into being until 2003. In theory, adding your number to this registry should stop telemarketers from calling you.

President Bush signed a bill authorizing the no-call list to go ahead in September 2003. As of October 1, 2003, it became illegal for most telemarketers or sellers to call a number listed on the National Do Not Call Registry. Registration for the Do-Not-Call list began on June 27, 2003, and enforcement started on October 1, 2003. Finally, the United States Court of Appeals for the Tenth Circuit on February 17, 2004, upheld the constitutionality of the law.[9] A survey, conducted less than a year after the Do Not Call list was implemented, found that people who registered for the list saw a reduction in telemarketing calls from an average of 30 calls per month to an average of 6 per month. You can see from the chart above we almost doubled in revenues from $7M in Q3, 2003, to $12M in Q3 2004.

When we made the management decision to recommend to the board to exit the custom marketing research it was June of 2001, about three months after I joined. The strategies we determined and executed to save the company were:

1. Finalize a cost effective method to continue to grow our online panel, the MSN River

2. Develop an effective sales process to convince the industry to use the new online data collection methods, and

3. Sell the business with the highest costs and online expertise and get enough cash to sustain our new business model.

We had to keep our recommendation quiet so the people working in the company on the custom projects wouldn't get nervous. Our goal was to sell that division and not have anyone lose their jobs. Too many people had already been negatively impacted and we needed to sustain the custom business so that it would continue to have a value and keep our hard-working people employed.

When we went to New York for our board meeting in June 2001, three months after I joined, we had pre-discussed the strategy with Peter Sobiloff and Jeff Horing from Insight Venture Partners. They loved the idea and were very supportive and promised to help get the others to follow along. It wasn't that easy. After all, more than $60 million had been invested in the business concept of doing customer marketing research by using an online panel as the differentiator. Harris Interactive went public on December 7, 1999, with a similar business model. The bubble had burst so the investors in Greenfield Online were confused and not quite sure the bubble days would not return. The conversation came down to the fact that they really had no choice if they didn't want to keep investing cash into the company.[10][11]

In the end we had to execute what is called in the venture world as a "cram down" or "down round." A down round doesn't indicate a company won't be successful in the future. It happens when a company raises funds by selling shares that are valued lower than the last time they raised funds.

This is taken from the S-1 filing document for the Harris Interactive IPO:

Companies are operating in an increasingly complex business environment, characterized by heightened competition, globalization of product markets, shortened product life cycles and rapidly changing consumer preferences. This business environment has escalated the need for accurate and timely information about the preferences, needs, purchase behavior and brand recognition of existing and potential clients. Companies also need continuous tracking capabilities so that they can ascertain product performance and competitive position, monitor consumer satisfaction, measure advertising effectiveness and determine price sensitivity. According to the European Society of Opinion and Marketing Research, $13.4 billion was spent for market research and polling services worldwide in 1998. Historically, information-gathering and tracking functions in market research have been performed using traditional market research methodologies.

The ability of traditional market research methodologies to deliver accurate and objective data rapidly is limited by high data acquisition costs, small sample sizes and the extensive time required to perform the research. As a result, broad-based research projects, which require a large number of survey participants, are prohibitively costly except for companies and organizations with significant resources. The growth and rapid adoption of the Internet is changing the market research and polling industry, making it possible for the first time to survey a very broad, diverse population at low cost and at speeds that are unattainable through any other method.

THE INTERNET AND ITS IMPACT ON THE MARKET RESEARCH AND POLLING INDUSTRY

The Internet has emerged as a mass communications and commerce medium enabling millions of people worldwide to gather and share information and conduct business electronically. International Data Corporation estimates that the number of Internet users worldwide will grow from 142 million at the end of 1998 to more than 500 million by the year 2003, and in the United States will grow from 63 million at the end of 1998 to 177 million by the year 2003.

The use of the Internet as a market research and polling tool is still in its infancy. Companies began the first testing efforts in 1995, at a time when less than 10 million persons in the United States had access to the Internet and the population on the Internet was not representative of the general population. We believe that, as Internet usage has increased, the demographic composition of those using the Internet has shifted to better reflect the characteristics of the overall population. As a result, with standard market research weighting procedures, the Internet is now a viable medium to conduct market research.

We believe that Internet-based market research and polling offers significant advantages over traditional methodologies. These include:

COST EFFICIENCY -- Internet-based market research and polling offers significant cost benefits when compared to traditional market research methodologies. Under traditional methodologies, the sample size of a survey is limited due to the high data collection costs per response.

However, utilizing Internet-based market research methods, larger and more robust sample sizes can be used for effectively the same cost, or the same sample size can be used to reduce the overall cost of a study.

VERSATILITY -- Internet-based market research combines the interactivity of telephone sampling with the visual capabilities of mail surveys. Pictures, graphics, advertising copy and other visual materials can be viewed over the Internet, a feature not available with telephone sampling. With Internet-based methodology, questions and their sequence in surveys can be modified as panelists respond. Mail panel surveys, in contrast, are limited to the order and content in the printed text of the survey.

SPEED -- Responses from online panelists are generally received within several days, while mail panelists' responses are generally received over several weeks. Further, when compared to a telephone survey, the speed advantage of the Internet model becomes greater as sample sizes increase.

PRODUCTIVITY -- The Internet is user-friendly to online panelists because surveys can be completed at the convenience of the participant and can be conducted 24 hours per day, seven days per week. In addition, because online panelists can read questions faster than they can listen, more questions can be asked to panelists in the same amount of time on the Internet than with traditional telephone survey methods. In our experience, a mail survey typically takes approximately six weeks from design to completion. In contrast, Internet surveys can generally be completed in two to seven days.[12]

This was true for Greenfield Online too. With our strategy change we were enabling *all* marketing research firms to offer online capabilities too. This would be a problem for Harris and we knew it. Suddenly their market advantage would go away. They were happy competing with a small startup like Greenfield Online but would not be happy to hear about our planned changes to enable all of their competitors to offer a similar method of collecting data online.

6

———⎯⎯⎯⎯⎯∽∾⎯⎯⎯⎯⎯———

The Summer
of 2001

Kantar Group, WPP plc, NFO Worldwide Inc., Taylor Nelson Sofres (TNS), and Harris Interactive were the primary targets to buy the Greenfield Online Customer Marketing Research Division. Bob, Jonathan Hugh, and I put a presentation together and set out to see what would happen. One of our first meetings was with Gordon Black, CEO of Harris Interactive. We knew that our strategy to separate the company would be a competitive threat to Harris. After all, we would be enabling all other traditional research firms to have a similar solution being offered by Harris. They also had an online panel and wouldn't need ours. The people and clients should have been interesting to them and it would have kept the rest of the industry from catching up to Harris's online survey data solutions. Gordon didn't seem to be very interested. I don't believe he thought we would survive. They did verbally offer to pay about $19 million and asked me to see if our investors would be interested.

As CEO I am obligated to bring any offer back to the board. Of course that offer would mean no one would make any money, and would only be a strategy to stop putting in any more cash. I wasn't sure how they would react. The offer was not in writing. Gordon just threw out a number to see our reaction. If they took it, it would be the end of my first CEO gig within six months and not a positive outcome. I knew we could do better. I was believing more and more each day in our Fieldsource business. It was logical and we were getting customers. I did pass along the verbal offer to the board and got the reaction I expected: "Ignore it."

My next meeting was with Eric Salama, CEO of Kantar at the time. We actually liked the team at Kantar and had high hopes that we could accomplish a deal. Kantar was a subsidiary of WPP and Eric was, in addition to his operating role at Kantar, the Strategy Director of WPP. The team at Kantar was headquartered a few miles away from Greenfield. We were in Wilton, and they were a few towns away. They also seemed to know most of our custom researchers and respected what Greenfield was attempting to do in the online survey world. Kantar was the parent organization of several research organizations and all needed online samples. Eventually they created their own company called Lightspeed to do much of what we were proposing to do with our Fieldsource business, except they would primarily only work with other Kantar research organizations. The meeting with Eric was a private dinner in New York. I believe they were seriously considering making an offer for Greenfield but it never came. One of the big problems we faced was that everyone knew we had been downsizing. The economy wasn't improving either so it was difficult for prospective buyers to offer much for our custom business. They would have been interested in getting the entire company and panel, but no price would come near the money already invested. All investors would take a huge loss. So we kept pitching.

Next was TNS. We drove to Horsham, Pennsylvania, near Philadelphia, to meet a team of senior managers and the CEO Bruce Shandler. The meeting went well and we quickly were delivered a term sheet. Bob, Jonathan, Hugh, and I did our best to work all of the interested parties to get us the best offer.

By late summer we were still struggling. Our Fieldsource business was hamstrung because the firms we wanted to sell to saw our custom research business as competitive and a potential threat. If they gave our Fieldsource team a project, they were afraid the custom team would contact the brand wanting the research and steal the work. We needed to move fast.

7

September 11, 2001

In the midst of what we thought were the worst business climate conditions during the summer of 2001, the world was reminded how precious life can be. Most people arrived at our Wilton offices between 8 A.M. and 9 A.M. each day. Wilton is a bedroom community where most residences commute into New York City each day. Our largest investor was on 5th Ave and 49th Street and most of their employees lived in the city.

Our modern office design had a TV screen in the lobby and another in the kitchen usually tuned to a news channel. Bob, Jonathan, and I each had TVs in our offices and also usually tuned to news. We never sat and watched them; they were mostly on for the atmosphere. On that Tuesday morning I remember hearing Jonathan scream from his office, pretty far away from mine, "Oh my God, we are under attack." Mind you, at the moment the first plane flew into the twin towers no one was reporting an attack. It was merely Jonathan's immediate reaction, which turned out to be amazingly correct. Everyone ran out of their offices and went to one of the TVs. Several of us ended up in Bob's office to watch the events unfold. The reporting was very uncertain as to what was happening as time went on. At 8:46:40: Flight 11 crashes into the north face of the North Tower (1 WTC) of the World Trade Center, between floors 93 and 99. The aircraft enters the tower intact. Remembering that day it seemed like a much longer time had passed from when Tower 2 was hit, but reports say that 9:03:00: Flight 175 crashes into the south face of the South Tower (2 WTC) of the World Trade Center, between floors 77 and 85. Parts of the plane, including the starboard engine, leave the building from its east and north sides, falling to the ground six blocks away. The entire office was fixated on the TV screens and we all watched in horror together as the second plane hit.

The week earlier Bob and I had been to the World Trade Center to meet with a few of our investors. Everyone in the office was now scrambling to get to a phone. The second plane and the reports of more hijackings created a sense of panic to reach their loved ones. No one knew what would happen next. I remember calling my ex-wife who lived in the Boston area with my son. It wasn't common knowledge yet that American Flight 11 and United Flight 175 both departed from Boston Logan airport. My ex-brother in law was a Massachusetts State Trooper stationed at Logan. My ex-wife was on the way to a dentist appointment with my son and made the decision to stop and turn around to get home as she heard the frightening news on the radio.

Once I made contact and knew they were safe I went back over to Bob's office and the kitchen to watch the events unfold for the day. We told everyone to feel free to head home to be with their loved ones, though there were many people who had still not heard from their inner circles to learn if their loved ones were safe. We were all in a state of shock and continued to be glued to TVs wherever we spent the night.

The next morning Greg Pierson came into my office. Greg is a special person to everyone who knows him. I got to know Greg because of his warm personality and his IT position with the company. Greg was originally hired by Hugh Davis. Greg was bartending at the Black Duck in Westport, Connecticut. Hugh lived in Westport and frequented "the Duck." As Greenfield started to grow, Hugh was always on the lookout for good people he could trust, regardless of experience. Greg was "trainable" and certainly had the right attitude about everything. A hard worker, helpful to everyone and anyone, and always with a positive attitude. When I joined, the company had been through multiple layoffs, the business climate was terrible, people were nervous about everything and Greg had a way of putting a smile on your face and making things seem better. As the IT guy he is the one that gave me my computer and got me connected, so to speak. I asked him to get me a Blackberry and to provide one to each of the management team. His response was that the company had some other "pagers" and that it wasn't a good idea for me to spend money on Blackberrys when we already had perfectly useful pagers. That was Greg. I tried to explain the difference. The next day he came to my office with a pager. I really enjoyed his attitude and boldness with his new CEO, but did insist on getting a Blackberry. Over the course of my first few months at the company Greg and I developed a special relationship. He was my ears to the ground so to speak. He would tell me things like, "You know, Dean, you should walk around the office more. The team needs to get to know you like I have."

The day after September 11, Greg walked into my office and said "Dean, we have all these computers in good working condition from the layoffs sitting in a room not being used. Why don't we donate them to the city and the rescuers? They could probably use them." That was Greg. My initial reaction was, Hey, we're a company that has been losing tons of money, so we can't make donations. But before he could object to a response like that, I caught myself and realized that this person is genuinely a good man. This is a great idea. Greg and a few others that worked with him loaded his van with over 20 computers and set off for a city in fear and police stopped all vans headed into the city. He made it in. Delivered them and set them all up so the rescue team had 20 additional working computers.

I will never forget that day or those following. Our employees had been through a great deal personally, prior to September 11, 2001. Now, in addition to experiencing the tragedies of living in one of the worst economic times, they survived the events of that day. We were focused on trying to save the business before 9/11, thinking almost

24/7 about how the impact of failure could mean devastation to our families when, when out of nowhere we learned a more valuable lesson about life. People really came together and were doing whatever they could to be supportive of the families directly impacted. Wilton lost four men that day. It seemed like everyone knew someone that had a direct loss.

8

The Deal

Six months after I joined as CEO the tragedy of September 11, 2001 occurred. Within ten months we sold the custom business to focus on Fieldsource. We did move fast and we were proud of our speed. Some say historical. On January 31, 2002 we signed an agreement with Taylor Nelson Sofres Intersearch Corporation. "TNS Operations" purchased from GFOL certain assets associated with GFOL's custom market research business (the "Custom Business").

From our S1 document filing in July of 2004 explaining the transaction, "TNSI agrees that the GFOL Sample Sources, and GFOL's proprietary software and technology used by GFOL in performing the GFOL Services, are and shall be solely owned by GFOL and shall constitute GFOL's confidential, proprietary, and trade secret information (the 'GFOL Property'). By entering into this Agreement or participating in the transactions described herein, TNSI shall not acquire any interest in and to any of the GFOL Property. Minimum Guaranteed Revenue: TNSI has committed to provide GFOL no less than $5,400,000 in revenue arising from the purchase of and payment for the GFOL Services as described in Section 1, during the first two years of the Term, the 'Minimum Guaranteed Revenue.'"

Not a bad deal by any measure. We saved the company by reducing expenses, getting some operating capital, and a guaranteed revenue stream for two years. Everyone in the Custom Research "division" was offered a job with TNS at the same pay and some more. No one lost their employment. The remaining Fieldsource "division" could now focus and the company could focus the Greenfield Online brand as the leading online platform for conducting marketing research. Actually brilliant.

As for monthly pre-payments, "TNS shall pre-pay its Minimum Guaranteed Revenue amount for each month of the first two years of the Agreement, between the first and fifth days (inclusive) of each calendar month, in the amount of $200,000 per month in the first year and $300,000 per month in the second year; provided that because the parties anticipate that TNSI's clients' demand for the GFOL Services will take several months to develop and mature from and after the execution of this Agreement."

At the time we were thrilled, but we had no idea how smart we were and how successful we would be. You can see in our audited financials pictured below that our provided "Internet Survey Solutions" sample to other marketing research firms went from $4 million in 2001 revenues to $14 million revenues in 2002. The custom research business ended for us when we sold it to TNS. Our gross profit in 2002 almost doubled with the same revenues in 2001. We went from a $9 million EBITDA loss in 2001 to a small EBITDA profit in 2002. We were off to the races. We had become one of the most successful business turnaround stories of all time.

Consolidated Statement of Operations Data:	2001	2002	2003
		($ in thousands, except per share data)	
Net revenues:			
Internet survey solutions(1)	$ 4,072	$14,416	$25,868
Custom research(2)	9,715	470	--
Total net revenues	13,787	14,886	25,868
Cost of revenues	8,097	5,409	8,884
Gross profit	5,690	9,477	16,984
Operating income (loss)	(14,213)	(3,908)	1,697
Total other income (expense)	(3,074)	945	101
Income (loss) before income taxes	(17,287)	(2,963)	1,798
Provision (benefit) for income taxes	--	(569)	150
Net income (loss)	(17,287)	(2,394)	1,648

9

Growing Fast

As we entered 2002 I hadn't even had my one-year anniversary. I was still living in an apartment across the parking lot from the office. My routine for the last year had been to drive from Wilton to North Andover, Massachusetts, on Friday evenings and return Sunday night or at dawn on Monday. This wasn't an ideal situation for any family but it was my choice to do what I could for my family by taking advantage of this opportunity. The drive was three hours each way. My apartment was nice with a garage. It was a two bedroom in the center of Wilton. When you're managing a growing startup the working hours are long anyway and I had a very easy daily commute to the apartment: a walk across the parking lot. I also had a Starbucks directly below my office. I am sure many of you reading this may find that to be a priceless company benefit, which I did find ideal. There was also a grocery store within walking distance too, probably under fifty yards from the Starbucks and one hundred yards from my apartment. I actually found this type of working situation very conducive for me to deal with the decisions we had to make at the company while we were growing fast.

One drawback was living alone and developing a kidney stone—the first of two episodes. My weight was always fluctuating and my diet was on and off. My first episode was terrifying. The intense pain that begins to develop deep inside your body is like nothing I had ever experienced. It was about 4 A.M. when I woke up with the pain. The fright made my mind search for a reason. Not only had I never experienced such pain, I had never experienced the frightening feeling of being helpless. I couldn't move. I rolled my body up into a fetal position to try to think if it would pass or if this was a life threatening experience. I wasn't about to call my ex-wife. What could she do three hours away? So I called Bob. I don't know why, I just didn't call an ambulance. I guess it was because Bob had become such a good friend and someone I knew I could count on. Bob's immediate response put me at ease. He said, "It sounds like a kidney stone. I will come get you." I honestly never knew anyone with a kidney stone or recognized the symptoms, I just felt like I could be near death.

The apartment was a two-story building, with the living area and bedrooms on the second floor. I crawled out of bed and stayed on the floor. There was no way I could stand or crawl, the pain was that severe. I slid myself down the stairs to the front door to wait for Bob to arrive. Maybe I knew he would be much faster than an ambulance because he got to me so fast. He did live close and he obviously didn't waste any time to get to me and drive me to the nearest hospital in Norwalk. As he pulled into the emergency area and I got out into a wheelchair a nurse immediately came to us and said "kidney stone." I spent the day in the hospital on morphine and liquids. I eventually passed the stone and was released.

Our employee count was less than half of what it was when I joined. We were feeling good and winning business. More and more research was moving to the Internet. We had cleared the way so marketing research organizations were no longer threatened by us having a competitive business. We were 100% focused on driving high-quality online respondents to surveys for our marketing research customers. Some of the big brands were attempting to build their own online panels, but the volume was such that they still needed us to collect the number of completed surveys they needed. We were doing business with every research company in the industry. A few competitors were cropping up, but for the most part we were at least asked to bid on every research project during 2002 that was conducted online.

Board meetings were jovial fun events. We didn't need any more cash because we were growing profitably and fast. Employees were working hard and enjoying seeing that their company had so much business they were required to work even harder. Their fears of losing their jobs had gone away.

Now we started to face a new problem: scaling to support our growth. Online surveys were proving to be better for many reasons, as explained by the following (from Wikipedia):

- Web surveys are faster, simpler, and cheaper.

- The entire data collection period is significantly shortened

- Interaction between the respondent and the questionnaire is more dynamic compared to e-mail or paper surveys. Online surveys are also less intrusive, and they suffer less from social desirability effects.

- Complex skip patterns can be implemented in ways that are mostly invisible to the respondent.

- Pop-up instructions can be provided for individual questions to provide help with questions exactly where assistance is required.

- Questions with long lists of answer choices can be used to provide immediate coding of answers to certain questions that are usually asked in an open-ended fashion in paper questionnaires.

- Online surveys can be tailored to the situation (e.g., respondents may be allowed save a partially completed form, the questionnaire may be preloaded with already available information, etc.).

- Online questionnaires may be improved by applying usability testing, where usability is measured with reference to the speed with which a task can be performed, the frequency of errors and user satisfaction with the interface.

We needed talented project managers to manage research projects for our customers. That meant keeping an eye on surveys as we selected panelists to be invited to take surveys. As demographic quotas would be reached we needed to redirect those people to other open surveys. We didn't want to "burn out" our panelist and we wanted to monetize those who responded so we needed more technology and people.

Most new survey projects get launched on Friday afternoons. Invitations would be sent to panelists and they would open their email and respond by clicking on a link to a survey. Once completed they would earn points and be asked to take another. We also offered the service of programming surveys so they could be run online for our marketing research customers. In those days they didn't have survey software readily available, or at least they were just learning about what was coming available for them to use. We needed more people to help us design software, more people to manage projects, more people to develop relationships like our MSN river to bring us more panelists. We also needed more sales people to book the sales with research organizations.

Keith Price, our original sales person for Fieldsource was promoted to be our Vice President of Sales in North America. We hadn't expanded to selling to Europe or Asia yet. We knew that in order to scale our sales team we needed to define our sales process so that it would be repeatable and trainable to new people when they joined the company. This meant a coordinated effort with marketing to help build the necessary messaging, white papers, webinar content, testimonials, and lead flow process into a pipeline to make our business more predictable. We began our search for a CRM solution and came across salesforce.com.

On March 8, 1999, in the apartment at 1449 Montgomery Street in San Francisco, the site of the first Salesforce office, the original gang of four employees gathered together. This group consisted of Benioff and Harris, and Harris's two programming colleagues, Dave Moellenhoff and Frank Dominguez. During 2001 we became an early adopter and I was asked to be a testimonial in a salesforce.com video. I was happy to do it. It became our single most important method to manage prospects, move them through our steps of the sales, deliver proposals and ultimately close and add new customers. Once their projects began, our services team would use the platform to manage all of the deliverables for the client. Our CFO, Bob Bies, relied heavily on the accuracy of the information and would track pipeline growth by stage. He built up historical data by week and by month, which allowed him to model our projections for future revenue attainment.

To drive adoption of our process and proper usage of Salesforce, we conducted Monday morning sales meetings without fail every week. Since the sales team was scattered around the country we conducted a conference call with a video share of the weekly reports. Each sales representative was responsible for reporting their pipeline growth by stage, proposals delivered, commitments made, and their personal forecast as to what they would close within the current month and quarter. Based on those numbers and personal projections and commitments, Bob was able to build weighted models that could get us to very accurate forecasts.

On the marketing side we would create sales supporting documents that the sales team could use depending on the type of work requested by the client. Since we were a new research methodology we created a lot of education material explaining why the Internet is better than telephone or face-to-face surveys. We created materials explaining the profile depth of our panelists so we can target and get quality results faster and cheaper. We had customers willing to explain how much faster we could deliver and with high-quality data.

Our sales strategy evolved to assign senior sales representatives to manage specific large research firms that spent at least $1 million a year with us and sometimes more. The concept was to help those firms win more business and become their online data collection expert.

In fiscal 2003, we derived approximately 27.1% of our total net revenues from two clients that accounted for approximately 14.5% and 12.7%, respectively. Our top client in 2003 was Taylor Nelson Sofres Intersearch (TNSI), with which we had an alliance agreement requiring it to make purchases of at least $5.6 million of our products and services from January 31, 2002, to January 31, 2004. TNSI satisfied this obligation and was no longer contractually required to purchase our products and services. In 2003, TNSI's parent company acquired NFO Worldgroup, Inc., which maintained and operated a large Internet respondent panel similar to our own. As a result of this acquisition, we expected the revenue we receive from TNSI in 2004 to be significantly less than in 2003. Our ten largest clients accounted for $13.8 million, or 53.4%, of our total net revenues for 2003. If we were to lose business from any of our top 10 clients, our net revenues would decline substantially.

We needed a senior level strategy that included me, Keith Price, Hugh Davis, Andy Ellis, and Bob Bies connected at the highest levels of our biggest clients. We planned quarterly meetings in person to review our company results, discuss areas to improve, and plan potential offerings that we could make proprietary to our biggest clients.

We had a great team of motivated managers across the company that built and managed their teams. There is nothing more fun and rewarding than success. It is great to be busy, and success does breed more success.

Keith Price, who was our first Fieldsource sales representative when I joined in 2001, reported to me the entire time I was CEO. Early on I asked Keith to run the Fieldsource sales team and eventually he became our global head of sales. Keith has had quite a career, and I am proud to have worked closely with him from 2001 until 2005 as our head of sales. Keith and the great team he built led the growth and scale that we were able to deliver. Keith eventually held the title of Executive Vice President at Greenfield Online, where he was responsible for global sales, operations, and marketing. Price was part of the management team and played a significant role in building Greenfield Online into a global, 600+ employee, publicly traded company. He was also instrumental in the ultimate sale of the business to the Microsoft Corporation in the fall of 2008 ($486 million) and Microsoft's sale of the survey division to Toluna in July 2009.

Andy Ellis joined early on and moved up to become Senior Vice President of Operations. Andy reported to Keith and led the operations team as we scaled globally. Now in 2020 Andy is Chief Revenue Officer at Lucid. Andy Ellis now has 15+ years experience managing global operations, sales, and technology teams in the market research industry. Andy joined Lucid as Senior Vice President of Corporate Development and transitioned into President of Federated Sample and Fulcrum, the original iterations of Lucid Marketplace. In March 2016, he became COO of Lucid. Before Lucid, Andy was Managing Director Europe and Asia-Pacific at Greenfield Online. He was part of the executive management team responsible for building them into a global, 600+ employee, publicly traded company as well as the ultimate sale of the business to Microsoft in 2008.

Alex Grinburg joined early to manage IT. He was IT Director in 2000 and eventually became our Chief Information Officer. David St Pierre joined as our CTO. Dave and I had worked together at Engage, and Dave was ideal to lead our scaling software development team. We had such great people including Mike Gaydos, Gina Lanzafama, Jenni Glaser-Cahalan, Danielle Quarrels, Frank Kelly, Val Karruck, Nelson Merchan, Nick Coelho, Neal Keltz, Marc McDonough, Doug Guion, Terence McCarron, Dave Gaston, Matt Nelson, Patty Smith, Tracey Jackson, Charles Pearson, Gina Pagano, Donald Panos, Cynthia Cronk, Drew Seath, Michael McCrary, and Gary Zucker. Forgive me for not naming everyone. Every area of the company experienced rapid growth due to our increase in sales, which meant more projects to be delivered, more sample needed, more surveys programmed, more data verified, and on and on. When preparing for the IPO, the accounting and finance departments as well as Jonathan Flatow, our in-house attorney, worked countless hours completing the necessary audits, legal documents, and the Security Exchange application. Jonathan was a practicing attorney in Westport when he was called on to work at the company. He joined Greenfield Online in March 2000 as the Company's Vice President of Corporate Development and General Counsel. In 2006, Jonathan was appointed Chief Administrative Officer. Jonathan played a key role in both Greenfield's IPO in 2004 the sale of Greenfield Online to Microsoft Corporation in 2008 for $500mm, at which time he was promoted to Chief Operating Officer.

We were having trouble finding enough people in Wilton. Our current employees were also being over worked and didn't like the late Friday and weekend hours. Bob, our CFO, was the first one to suggest investigating adding people offshore. In 2002 offshore outsourcing was happening but just getting started. We had determined that a project manager job to be filled in Wilton was about $80,000 a year plus benefits and a person with similar qualifications could be found offshore for about $30,000. Times have changed and today that is no longer the case, but in 2002 we set out to investigate if this was true.

One of the benefits of Insight Venture Partners was their network of people. They organized a conference style meeting with their portfolio company management to discuss topics of interest to each of us. One of the sessions included Robert Rubin, former cabinet member, and retired banking executive. He served as the 70th United States Secretary of the Treasury during the Clinton administration. He spoke at the conference and I was invited to be one of a few others to join him for dinner. We had an open discussion about the topic of hiring people offshore and I was able to present our situation. His public political position was against offshore development. Privately, he understood the challenges businesses face and to create shareholder value and increase profits it is necessary to add offshore capabilities. Our business model and valuation of the company would improve dramatically if we could deliver more survey projects and collect data with high gross margins and ultimately bottom line profit. It wasn't that we weren't faithful to our country. We were responsible business managers and had to make the right choice for our company. The decision actually enabled us to sell more and eventually create more positions in the United States.

Expanding our staff in India was an option. Some of the benefits of doing this were that due to the time change the people there could work the same hours as Eastern Standard Time and we could add shifts that could provide us 24/7 coverage on research projects for our customers. We could take a survey designed by one of our customers in the U.S. and send it to our office in India to be programmed for online and have it ready by the next morning for our customer to test: an amazing service for our industry and a very strategic market leading decision for us. We began looking for a General Manager to open and run our offshore operation outside Delhi.

Our first explorer of this decision, and logical choice, was Greg Pierson. We asked Greg to make the trip to Delhi and investigate what it would take to open an office there. We also hired a consultant to assist us. Greg had never been to India, but he knew what our facilities would require, and he was a great project manager with great people skills. We knew he would be a great ambassador. I wish I had saved an email Greg had sent to Bob, Jonathan, and me after he arrived in Delhi and spent a few days there. It went something like this: "The hotel I am staying in wouldn't be suitable for you. The vodka that I brought with me is being used to soak my toothbrush and I use it for mouthwash. I see a great deal of poverty and cattle running through the streets. I don't understand why they aren't feeding their people. As for finding good talent, I met with several people who responded to our survey programmer advertisement. We had almost one thousand responses. There are more than one billion people here and many who have had a great education and speak perfect English. Microsoft and Bank of America have offices in a building that has space available for us."

We started our office there in early 2003 and quickly expanded. CK (Chandra) Taneja Ph.D., MBA, and MCA was hired as our General Manager in Gurgaon, a city just southwest of New Delhi in northern India. It's known as a financial and technology hub. We eventually added sample management, survey programming, panel management and panel acquisition positions there and grew to more 200 people by 2004. We reduced our costs and speed of delivery to our customers, which fueled our growth nicely. We were able to double the number of projects delivered each year, from 1,249 in 2002 to 2,482 in 2003. Our revenues grew from $14,416 million in 2002 to $25,868 million in 2003 and an EBITDA profit of 14% within three years of my joining the company.

Our employee base had grown from 54 in February 2002 to approximately 190 as of April 5, 2004, including employees of our subsidiaries in India, the United Kingdom, and Canada. The recruiting, hiring, training, and integration of a large number of employees throughout the world placed a significant strain on our management and operational resources. We had to successfully develop, implement, maintain, and enhance our financial and accounting systems and controls, integrate new personnel and manage expanded operations to effectively manage our growth.

My first trip to India was a great experience. I wished I had made it sooner. After all, the team we added there was passionate about helping the company succeed, and they truly wanted to show the positive impact they believed they could deliver for us. We grew there rapidly and the team was very excited about the opportunity. I arrived late in the evening around 11 P.M. local time and had a driver waiting with his Mercedes for me. He was my caretaker for the week I was there. We arrived at my hotel about an hour from the airport. The ride was an interesting one. Even though the time was approaching midnight, the traffic was slow and the highway was full. It was full of people walking, riding bicycles, motor scooters, one scooter with six people on it, an elephant, cars, trucks, buses and cows. The hotel had a high wall around the entire property and the gate was very tall and made of iron. As we drove in there were many uniformed bellmen, beautiful landscapes, and fountains. A true five-star experience was my initial impression. When I got to my room it was appointed as nice as any five-star hotel in the U.S. The refrigerator was stocked with plenty of bottled water.

When I got to our office I was pleasantly surprised. We were in a complex with Microsoft and Bank of America. We were adding people at a fast rate, and in less than two years were over 150 people in India.

CK, our general manager, was very experienced and had worked in the U.S. and had also run large teams in India. He guided us on what we needed to do to hire, retain, and motivate good people. He built a great team and enabled us to grow. We made a deliberate effort to make everyone in the company feel connected, and one of our methods was to use video conferencing as often as possible. We had people travel from our corporate offices every month to work there and stay a minimum of two weeks. We asked Doug Guion and Greg Pierson to spend extended time there, which was priceless for our ability to train, motivate, and build cohesive teams. Our U.S. personnel relied on our people in India to deliver our projects to our customers. We also brought people to the U.S. from time to time. During one visit to the U.S. several of our India employees got to experience the Red Sox–Yankee baseball rivalry first hand. Well, almost first hand. You remember the description of the conference room next to my office with a large screen dropdown projection unit and surround sound? Half of us were Red Sox fans and the others were Yankees fans. The conference room was packed, we ordered in lots of food, and watched the game together. It was a 2003 playoff game and it delivered the typical rivalry game excitement.

There were many things we did there to help our employees. We had drivers with cars to pick up and drive people to work in the morning and home at night. A car wasn't necessary for employees. My first night there, I came out of the office and noticed at least 20 to 30 drivers, each with a Mercedes, standing around waiting for people to come outside so they could drive them home. We had people all day in the office who would walk up and down the cube rows offering water to everyone. That was their entire job.

We had a company party while I was there to recognize the great progress and individual contributions. The party was in a hotel ball-room with a band, videographer, photographer, and a buffet for 100 people including their families. The total cost was under $10,000. We even had white chair covers and tablecloths.

I was treated like a king. My fondest memories were of our employees and their families and how warmly they welcomed me to their country. We were like a big family and it was truly genuine. After my speech and delivering the awards the music continued at a club-like pace. I was swept on to the dance floor and really didn't have time to notice that it was a group of men that were all dancing together. I just started to move like they did and had a great time.

My time there was two short, only a week. I did get a tour of Delhi and witnessed the poverty. I believe our team there wanted to be sure that my only memories of my trip were good ones and kept me from seeing too much of the negative, but it is impossible to avoid when you are in India.

10

Growing Faster

By the end of 2003 we had grown to $25 million in revenues. In 2000 we had $2 million in revenues from our Internet Solution, in 2001 we had $4 million, in 2002 we had $14 million and in 2003 we had $25 million. We delivered 14% EBITDA margins in 2003 or $3.6 million, earnings before interest, taxes, depreciation, and amortization (EBITDA). In 2001 the company had a negative EBITDA loss of $38 million. A nice turnaround! We were so busy working and growing the business we never stopped to look at the great accomplishments. We knew everyone was happy, but the financial reporting usually trails the actual operations, so the final 2003 results were not audited until February, 2004.

Bob and I were in the office late as usual and we decided to listen to the earnings call of Harris Interactive. When they reported their results we looked at each other. We were more profitable and growing faster than Harris! The analyst from Piper Jaffrey who covered Harris was asking a few questions, so we got his name. When the call ended, Bob said, "Let's call him." We did and he answered. We had him on the speakerphone in my office and told him who we were and why we were calling. After Bob ran through our results with the analyst he said, "You guys need to speak with our bankers. They would be interested in taking you public. Those are amazing results."

We went to the next board meeting in February of 2004 and told the members about our call with Piper Jaffrey. They approved our recommendation to begin a process to select a lead banker to investigate an IPO for Greenfield Online. This was a whole new world to me and probably is to everyone that gets into this similar position. I heard that there are approximately 3,500 people who have led initial public offerings and I was going to be one of them. During the immediate years following the bubble burst in 2001 the number of IPOs was very small. The laws tightened and the process required more scrutiny, which increased the costs for a company to go public. Bob and Jonathan had been through the process before in 1999 when the company was attempting the IPO the first time.

In 2004 Google, Dreamworks and Salesforce were three other companies to do an IPO. We began meeting with bankers in February and had made a decision to go with Lehman Brothers as our lead, with Piper Jaffrey and Friedman Billings Ramsey as our two other supporting banks. It was very competitive. We chose these three because we thought Goldman Sachs and Morgan Stanley were too big and we would get lost. We also liked the experience of Lehman Brothers, and the analysts at Piper and Friedman knew our industry well. These are the banks that make the market and create the demand. The lead bank runs the show. Our attorneys were Gary J. Kocher and Michael W. Moyer from Preston Gates & Ellis LLP in Seattle, Washington. They were the firm that represented Microsoft. Also, Raphael M. Russo of the firm Paul, Weiss, Rifkind, Wharton & Garrison LLP, New York, NY 10019.

Representatives from these companies and our auditors practically lived in our offices from March to July of 2004. The writing of the Form S-1 Registration Statement required countless hours of writing and review. If you're familiar with those documents, you know they present the business as well as the financial data. It is also supposed to declare all of the potential risks for potential investors to read before buying shares. Our S-1 was over 100 pages. This is the "overview" from the actual S-1 filing form:

"We are a leading independent provider of Internet survey solutions to the global marketing research industry and we derive 100% of our revenues from Internet data collection products and services. We actively manage the Greenfield Online panel, a 100% Internet-based panel of approximately 1.7 million individuals who participate in our surveys. Our panelists represent households consisting of an estimated 4.7 million people, allowing us to compile diverse, demographically representative survey data.

We target our Internet survey solutions to approximately 2,500 full service marketing research and consulting firms in the United States and the world's top 25 marketing research companies. Our clients use the Internet survey data that we provide to enable companies throughout the world to make critical business decisions. Based on our internal estimates, we believe that spending associated with the gathering of survey data, known as fieldwork, accounts for approximately 40% of the annual spending on survey marketing research. Using this estimate, fieldwork represented approximately $3.0 billion of the $7.5 billion global survey market in 2002 as reported by the *World Association of Opinion and Marketing Research Professionals.*

"Until January 2002, we sold both custom Internet-based marketing research and the Internet survey solutions we sell today. A majority of our revenues for the first seven years of the company's existence was derived from the sale of custom research. In September 2001, we embarked on a strategy to convert the focus of our business from providing custom research to end-users to providing Internet survey solutions to the marketing research firms we target today. This strategy culminated in the sale of our custom research business in January 2002. This sale represented a turning point in our development as we shifted from a labor-intensive, professional services model to a scalable, Internet-based services model.

"Greenfield Online's sales strategy became a strategy to partner with marketing research firms that became our clients to leverage their global sales forces and not compete with them for custom marketing research business. This cooperative marketing strategy led to significant market penetration. For the year ended December 31, 2003, we completed 2,482 Internet-based projects, a 99% increase over 2002. Additionally, 45 companies each purchased over $100,000 of our products and services in 2003, an 88% increase over 2002.

Internet survey solutions are faster, more efficient, and more cost-effective for collecting high-quality marketing research data than traditional, labor-intensive methods such as telephone, direct mail, and mall-based surveying. The Internet allows our panelists to participate 24 hours a day in a more convenient and less intrusive environment than traditional data collection methods. Our Internet-based technology interactively engages respondents through the use of images, sound and video, enabling us to collect richer data for our clients. We believe Internet-based survey solutions speed survey completion, allow for significantly larger survey sample sizes over a given time period and provide marketing researchers with a cost-effective means of reaching niche segments.

"We believe we are well positioned to capitalize on evolving dynamics within the global survey research market. Decreasing cooperation rates experienced by the telephone survey industry and the increasing use of mobile phones as a primary means of telephone communication have led to a decline in the effectiveness of traditional telephone-based data collection methods. This decline has been exacerbated by the recently established Do Not Call registry, covering over 58 million telephone numbers. At the same time, Internet penetration rates and increased broadband usage have accelerated growth in the use of Internet-based marketing research. We believe these dynamics will drive demand for our Internet survey solutions. Through our North American operations, sales offices in the United Kingdom and Continental Europe and our production facilities in India, we believe we are well-positioned to meet this demand."

Once we made our banker selections we had to convince them we would continue to see the growth we had recently delivered. We ended 2003 at $25.8 million in revenue up from $14.4 in 2002. The basis for people wanting to buy our stock would be primarily based on top-line growth and the conversion of the data collection methods for marketing research from primarily telephone surveys to online surveys. We expected our 2004 results to be over $40 million. The regulators require a company to be profitable for at least a year and in 2003 and we had accomplished that metric. We also had strong growth and were forecasting continued growth during 2004. After weeks of working around the clock Bob and Jonathan and our finance team, auditors, and lawyers completed our application and filed to wait for approval. Once the application is filed with the Securities Exchange Commission (SEC) you don't know for sure how long it will take to get through the process or if there will be questions that need to be answered. Once approved the company enters into a "quiet period" where no one is allowed to talk to the press, make public statements or discuss the IPO. While waiting for approval we worked on our investor presentation. This is the 20- to 30-minute "pitch" the CEO and CFO make to investors while on the "road show" to build up interest ahead of the IPO day.

We had experienced significant growth in our revenues related to Internet survey solutions since 2000. Starting with a base annual revenue of $2.1 million in 2000, our Internet survey solutions revenues grew to $25.9 million for the year ended December 31, 2003. The following chart depicts growth of our quarterly services revenues derived from Internet survey solutions from January 2001 through December 2003. You can see in the chart below that in Q1, Q2, Q3, and Q4 of 2001, my first quarters at the company, there was little growth until we got out of the custom research business in Q1 of 2002. It was January of 2002 that we closed the sale of the custom business to TNS and focused the company on a single business objective.

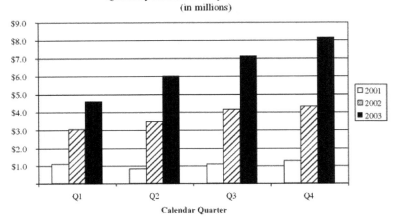

Quarterly Internet Survey Solutions Revenue
(in millions)

11

Going Public

O ur financial performance, together with the industry change from telephone research to online research, positioned us well for an IPO. Our presentation was built on that. These are some of the slides taken directly from the presentation we literally gave more than 150 times in two weeks.

Changing an Industry via the Internet

Industry	Status Quo	Internet Revolutionary	New Paradigm
	Travel agencies dominated, disintermediation rules	Expedia.com	Buy tickets, rent cars, book hotel rooms online, power shifts to consumer
	Big box stores, malls, retail outlets	amazon.com	One click to purchase, buy online via credit cards
	Record stores selling entire CDs		File sharing shakes up industry, model is evolving to buying songs for $0.99
	Newspapers, classifieds, flea markets, auctions	ebY	The most successful online business has become the largest online marketplace
	Paper resumes & experience search firms	monster	Electronic resumes, employer & employee screening tools
	Costly, inefficient, inaccurate	Greenfield	High quality, cost effective data collection

Greenfield
ONLINE

Like the other companies listed, Expedia, Amazon, Apple, eBay, and Monster, we were changing an industry by the Internet too.

Investment Highlights

- Revolutionizing data collection in the $18 billion Marketing Research Industry

- 100% Internet-based business model with significant operating leverage
    - Low variable costs as a % of revenue, high FCF conversion ratio of 81%

- Favorable regulatory and communications trends

- Active survey panel of 1.7 million households, ~ 4.7 mm individuals

- Proven results: revenue and EBITDA growth for 9 consecutive quarters
    - 74% revenue growth 2003 vs. 2002, 17% EBITDA margins and growing

The Foundation of Marketing Research

Greenfield ONLINE

Confidential

6

The marketing research industry spent more than $18 billion a year on data collection. In 2004 only 15% or so of the industry was using the Internet for survey data collection. The primary method was still telephone or face-to-face surveys. We had a long way to go to lead the industry conversion to the Internet. Over the last several decades the industry has migrated from personal interviews to telephone interviews to direct mail surveys to interviewing people in the malls and automated machine dialing systems for conducting interviews. It was time for the Internet. People could answer questions when they wanted, not when they were interrupted and we could invite the types of people we needed to reach because we knew more about them in our panel. Based on the information we collected in the past and their decision to participate, we could track profiles and attributes about them, age, ailment, zip code, education, etc.

Migration to Internet Based Marketing Research

50's – Personal Interviews	60's – Telephone Interviews	70's – Direct Mail Surveys	80's – Mall Based Surveys	90's – Automated Phone Interviews	**2000's + Internet Surveys**

Marketers had questions and we had answers. If we were making this slide today we would add smartphones and social media to the migration path of data collection for marketing research purposes.

Marketers Have Questions.
Greenfield Gets Them Answers.

Representative Company	Representative Question	Type of Study	Answers
GM	• How is the Chevrolet brand perceived by 18-35 year old women on the west coast who are purchasing cars within the next 6 months?	Brand Tracking Study	
P&G	• Will customers be responsive to this product and its packaging?	Shelf Testing	
FOX	• How will audiences respond to this movie trailer? What percentage of the audience would go see the film?	Media Testing	

Greenfield ONLINE ————————— Confidential —————— 8

Historical methods lost their effectiveness. This was our industry's "perfect storm." The Do Not Call legislation enabled people to block telephone solicitation and effectively drive the conversion from phone surveys to the Internet. At the same time, mobile phones were growing at very fast adoption rates and more and more people were canceling their landline service in the home. To complete the picture was our ability to charge less. On average, a general population survey charged $12.50 per completed survey. The mall was $32 each and telephone was $20. So faster, better, cheaper was true. The "better" was debated by scholars and those with something to lose by the move of data collection to the Internet. The non-Internet methods were one dimensional, inconvenient, inefficient, and had interviewer bias. We could imbed multimedia in the online survey, complete them whenever/wherever with targeted capabilities and eliminate bias. We could literally complete our surveys in hours and other methods would take weeks.

Historical Methods Have Lost Their Effectiveness

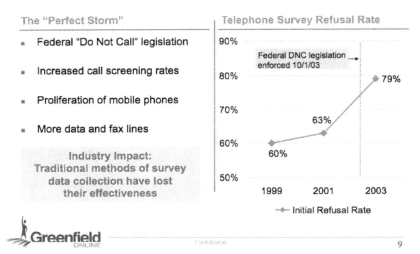

The "Perfect Storm"	Telephone Survey Refusal Rate
▪ Federal "Do Not Call" legislation	
▪ Increased call screening rates	
▪ Proliferation of mobile phones	
▪ More data and fax lines	

Industry Impact:
Traditional methods of survey
data collection have lost
their effectiveness

Greenfield ONLINE

Confidential

9

We had become the center of the marketing research industry value chain. The chain typically began with a product in development and market intelligence was needed from end users. The marketing research firm would sell their services of designing a survey that would ultimately help them draw the right conclusions, help them define the target sample, and manage the data collection and deliver their analysis. The brand or buyer of the research would then make a decision. Greenfield Online would program the survey, invite our panelists to take the survey, validate it, and report to the research firms.

The Center of the Internet Marketing Research Value Chain

Greenfield Online Internet Survey Solution

We were the foremost player in the fastest-growing segment of the marketing research industry. Our online panel of 1.7 million U.S. households was 100% "double opt-in." This means that once they told us that they wanted to join the panel, we would send an email asking them to confirm that they really wanted to join. Our competitive differentiator was that we had superior response rates due not only to the verification that they meant to join, but because we got their permission to collect profile data that enabled us to target specific people. For example, not only did we know their sex, race, education, marital status, we also knew if they had high blood pressure or athlete's foot. We developed specialty panels of physicians, mothers with babies, and other people who intended to purchase automobiles in the next year. We had been managing the online panel since 1994 with zero marketing to panel, superior technology infrastructure, specialized incentive programs and full-time panel managers.

Our strategy has been very focused since 2002. Drive migration of traditional fieldwork to our Internet survey solutions:

99

- Increase size and diversity of Greenfield online panel
- Develop new and innovative Internet survey solutions
- Grow international business
- Create demand by building the premier Pan European panel
- Pursue strategic acquisitions using offering proceeds and stock
- Geographic and panel expansion
- Accelerate time to scale

Foremost Player in the Fastest Growing Segment of Marketing Research

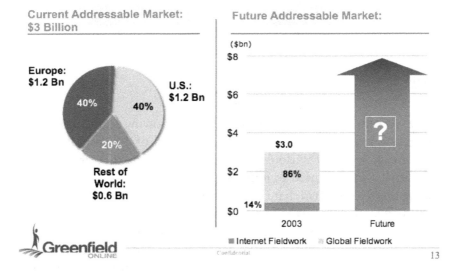

We were extremely proud of our financial performance. Bob would deliver the presentation of the numbers. Not only were we coming off a great year of revenue growth of 74%, $14.9 million to $25.9 million, we were delivering an 81% free cash conversion in 2003.

Growth Driven by Shift to 100% Internet Survey Solutions Model

Annual Revenue

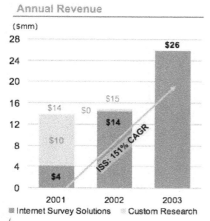

($mm)

2001	$4, $10, $14
2002	$0, $14, $15
2003	$26

ISS: 151% CAGR

■ Internet Survey Solutions   Custom Research

Financial Summary

Metric	2002	2003
Revenue	$14.9	$25.9
EBITDA	0.2	4.3
EBITDA Margin	1%	17%

- Strong growth in 2003 vs. 2002
  - 74% Revenue growth
- 81% FCF conversion in 2003

Greenfield
ONLINE

Confidential

18

As we were about to hit the road for the IPO in July of 2004 we had delivered $8.6 million in revenue compared to $4.6 million a year ago in Q1, 2003. Our growth was continuing and we had no reason to believe it would slow down. In fact, our growth rate increased to 88% in 2004 versus 61% for the same quarter a year ago. We accomplished that with incremental sales, no acquisitions, just selling more and delivering more. The entire company was executing as a team, and everyone was busy quoting project prices, closing sales, programming surveys, inviting panelists to take them, checking the data, and delivering the results to our clients. We had to keep the flow of new panelists, make sure we didn't burn out the ones we had, and keep the surveys to a reasonable length. In fact, that was one of our biggest challenges. We once laughed how we had a marketing research firm ask us if we had people with attention disorder in our panel and could we get them to take a one-hour survey? Seriously.

Proven Results: Track Record of Growth

Quarterly Revenue

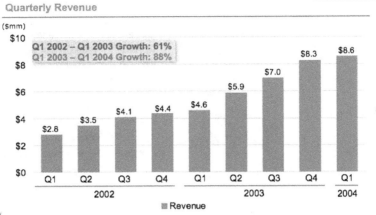

Greenfield
ONLINE

Confidential

19

Incremental Operating Leverage

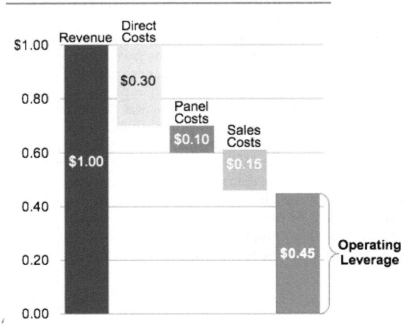

Bob's favorite slide and topic was "our operating leverage." For every additional $10 million of revenue that we could generate we would increase our EBITDA by $4.5 million. Our business model had 30% direct costs, 10% panel costs, 10% selling costs, and 45% operating leverage.

We practiced the presentation in front of our board, the bankers, and attorneys more times than I can remember. During the waiting period Lehman Brothers asked me if I would like to meet one of their bankers, John Kasich. I was familiar with John Kasich and his accomplishments as the House of Representatives Chairman of the House Budget Committee (he was also a host at that time of a program on Fox called "Heartland"[13]).

In 1995, when Republicans gained the majority in the United States Congress following the 1994 election, Kasich became chairman of the House Budget Committee. Of course I wanted to meet Mr. Kasich and was thrilled to be in a position to have a one-on-one dinner with him. We had the chance to spend time getting to know each other at a restaurant in Manhattan. Here was a man who had accomplished so much in his life, sitting with me having a private dinner!

Among other things we discussed, Kasich told me that after attending public schools in his hometown of McKees Rocks, he later left his native Pennsylvania, settling in Columbus, Ohio, in 1970 to attend the Ohio State University.

As a freshman, he wrote a letter to President Richard Nixon describing concerns he had about the nation and requesting a meeting with the president. The letter was delivered to Nixon by the University's president Novice Fawcett, and Kasich was granted a 20-minute meeting with Nixon in December 1970. He told me how he had a chance to intern one summer at the White House but his family had no ability to cover his costs and costs weren't included in the internship offer. He set off for Washington, D.C., by bus and found a dorm living room at American University, where he could sneak some sleep. (Coincidentally, after I attended Ithaca College for my freshman and sophomore years, I transferred to American University in Washington, D.C.) In 1993, Kasich became the ranking Republican member of the House Budget Committee.

To return to the issues surrounding the IPO, we waited for approval of our application from the Security Exchange Commission. It eventually came. The bankers recommended that we spend a week in Europe making presentations prior to the official US roadshow. We didn't object.

We went public on Nasdaq on July 15, 2004. We left for Europe in June to "practice," but we were actually presenting in front of potential investors and hoped to generate excitement and enthusiasm for buyers of our stock. We boarded a Lufthansa flight that was entirely business class. This would be the first of many over the next few years. I met Bob at the airport and the two bankers from Lehman brothers. Bob, who hadn't traveled extensively over the immediate preceding years, showed up with a suitcase the size of a Volkswagen. We were planning to be gone for two weeks, so while we did need a lot of clothes I'd never seen a suitcase that large. As we went down the runway and started to climb into the air, Bob and I sat next to each other, reclined, and waited for our service to begin. We enjoyed a great meal and a few glasses of wine. As I rolled on to my side to try to get a few hours of sleep I felt Bob's arm wrap around my shoulder. He "spooned me!" and we broke into hysterical laughter. Bob had an amazing sense of humor and our exciting trip was about to begin after three amazing years. We were starting to enjoy the adventure as friends who had shared circumstances from having no cash for payroll, to witnessing 9/11, to changing our company business model, selling the custom research division, growing sales and profits—and now on a plane to start our IPO roadshow.

I wish I had kept a diary of the stops and where we presented. I know we visited London, Milan, Munich, and Monte Carlo for a weekend excursion. The meetings were generally a group of five to ten investors at a time in very posh offices. I remember Milan mostly because Bob went shopping to fill his giant suitcase with gifts for his wife and two daughters. That is why he had such a huge suitcase.

Since we had a stay over the weekend and the bankers were paying, we chose to spend it in Monte Carlo. We actually booked a round of golf at the Monte Carlo Country Club. Who could imagine you could have a golf course on the side of a mountain, but there is, and every hole is either going up or down a hill. When we arrived in Monte Carlo we needed a helicopter to take us to our hotel. The helicopters had room for the pilot and two passengers with normal-sized suitcases. Bob's giant bag wouldn't fit no matter how hard we tried. The pilot, Bob, and I all made a group effort to lift, turn, and move in all directions to see if there was any way possible to get it inside with room for us. Impossible. The pilot took us to the hotel and went back to make a special trip just for Bob's bag. As we stood there at the landing area waiting we had a good laugh, but when we saw the helicopter on the horizon with a rope hanging from it and about twenty feet below the helicopter was Bob's suitcase at the end of the rope. As he got to the landing area the helicopter had to hover while one of the ground helpers went to rescue the bag and untie it from the helicopter. Once untied, the pilot never landed; he just went back to the airport with a wave while laughing.

I also can't remember all of the stops we made in the U.S. This was my first experience on a private jet, also paid for by the banker. It is the only way to fly or travel, period. You have a car pick you up at your home or hotel and drive you to the private section of the airport, get out of your car, and walk on to your own private plane. Ours was a Hawker 800.

The **Hawker 800** is a mid-size twinjet corporate aircraft.

I do remember one of the stops in Houston. It had been a long day and we landed late after dark. We hopped into a taxi and told the driver the name of the hotel we were staying at. He responded: "Do you know which side of the hotel you are on?" Bob and I looked at each other, and we could tell by looking at each other that he was asking an odd question. As we pulled up we answered simultaneously "no" and before we could ask why, he said be sure to ask for the north side. As we got to the front desk I asked the agent if we could both get "north side rooms?" The agent responded, "Sorry, those are sold out but we have very nice south side rooms for both of you." We were tired and took our keys and went to our rooms.

I generally sleep commando style, quickly brushed my teeth, and climbed into my king bed. I was exhausted and fell into a deep sleep immediately. Suddenly, I was awakened by the sound of a glass-shattering horn blast as though it was held one inch from my head. As I jumped to my feet stark naked, my eyes were drawn to the curtains where a bright light was shining so brightly I thought the sun was crashing to Earth and about to hit my window. I raced to the window and through open the curtains, standing there stark naked looking at a train headed straight toward me and my window. I froze. Luckily, the train tracks ran under my hotel and within a few minutes my panic would be gone because the train disappeared between my legs and under the building. This went on every hour of the night.

I believe we brought a case of wine for the journey. From that day on I know we had a glass or two each night. Each day we were asked what we wanted for food and drinks. They would cater it with whatever we wanted. The last day we asked for a bucket of Kentucky Fried Chicken.

We made more than 150 presentations in a three-week period. That is an average of making the same presentation more than ten times a day, sometimes to one person and other times to a room full of people. It was grueling but no complaint came from me.

Greenfield Online—its ticker would be SRVY—priced its initial public offering of 5 million shares at $13 each late Thursday, July 15, 2004, for proceeds of $65 million.

Almost as soon as we finished the initial public offering, we were being asked by our investors to do a secondary offering. That is the same process again to raise more money for the company and to help investors sell some of their shares. The IPO was in July 2004 and the secondary was in December of 2004.

When you raise money in the public markets you're expected by the investors to spend it and utilize it to help grow the business. Our primary need was having a continuous flow of people to take surveys online, and we needed to stay ahead of our competitors not only with the broadest panel but with a global one. My role evolved from saving the business, building the teams across the company from sales, sample, operations, technology and administration, to communicating to stock analysts, investors, and owners of potential acquisition targets.

12

Reaching a $400 Million Valuation

We were constantly talking among ourselves about ideas for acquiring companies. One of the challenges a company faces is how the thought or discussions about buying other companies immediately impacts all employees. Most begin to focus on their roles and how they may change. We tried to keep the strategic discussions between Bob, Jonathan, and me, but we needed Hugh, Keith, Janice, Alex, and Andy to give us their perspectives. After all, they were closest to our customers and what our competitors were doing. We had every competitor as a potential target. Since we were in a new industry and the leader of it, we had the attention of every competitor. If they were trying to find investors, we created a nice comparison for them based on our valuation. We in essence caused the value of our competitors to rise just based on our success and value we created. We established a public market price.

My number one target was E-Rewards. They had built a great panel of business people via a relationship with American Airlines.

Companies with products and services for business people would pay more for each survey. That demographic generally avoids taking surveys or simply doesn't have time. They would respond if rewarded with airline miles, and E-Rewards was probably our fastest-growing competitor due to having access to business consumers. The travel industry, hotels, car rental, airlines would love to be able to survey business travelers. They also knew what loyalty club the panelist belonged to and could ask questions about competitors if they chose to ask. This was a very valuable panel and a segment of the business where we were weak.

I tried to develop a relationship with Hal Brierly, the founder. Hal was a very experienced and successful businessman. From *D Magazine*, a magazine that covers the Dallas–Fort Worth area of Texas: "In 1980, a former classmate from Harvard hired Brierley to design American Airlines' traveler rewards program. Brierley later became the vice president of sales and marketing for Pan American World Airways in 1982, where he developed the WorldPass loyalty program. After a year at Pan Am, Brierley, left to become the senior vice president of marketing for Continental Airlines. Initially founded in 1999 in Dallas Texas by Hal Brierley and Mort Meyerson, the company was called E-Rewards, Inc.[14] E-Rewards had grown fast to over 100,000 clients in a just few months." Their method of attracting panelists was superior. They were able to attract business travelers through their relationship with American Airlines. Lots of money is spent each year attempting to research business people, but we didn't have that demographic.

Looking back, I regret not making this happen. Today, in 2020, E-Rewards has become one of the leading companies in the marketing research data-collection industry. In December 2009, "E-Rewards, Inc. acquired Research Now Plc,[15] which was co-founded by Chris Havemann and Andrew Cooper, and headquartered in London, England. At the time, Research Now was publicly listed on the London Stock Exchange's AIM market. Through the integration process, the company re-branded globally under one name as Research Now. The company went on to acquire some other smaller businesses including Peanut Labs, Inc., between 2010–2015.

In January 2015, private equity firm Court Square acquired Research Now Group Inc.[16] At a similar time, private equity firm HGGC had acquired a majority stake a rival market research firm, Survey Sampling International (SSI), and in 2017, the two PE firms announced they would be merging the two market research firms. In January 2019, the combined Research Now SSI was renamed to Dynata.[17]

Hal had a great team of people working with him selling and delivering. Hal and I even discussed a price for the company, which I believed was too high for me to convince our board to approve. I moved on to the next targets, Rapidata and goZing.

Rapidata was a company that enabled pharmaceutical market researchers to access health care providers and their patients for marketing research purposes. The deal would make Greenfield Online one of the only survey solutions providers with deep online panel ownership across a broad range of health care provider specialties. We saw strong demand and a willingness to pay a much higher price for the ability to target specific people by ailment or drugs used. Individuals were willing to provide that information and get compensated for answering questions. For example, we could deliver to researchers overnight a representative sample of people with type A diabetes. Greenfield paid $5.5 million in cash for the acquisition. This was a good first acquisition for us to use the money we raised in the public markets. We could grow our panel, sales, and add high-margin capabilities and further identify our company as the leading online sample provider for marketing research. We also added a qualified experienced team. (Ben Feldman, Rapidata's chief executive, and Jay Mebane, Rapidata president, later became vice presidents of Greenfield Online.)

I stated the following in our press release announcing the acquisition:

> "Health care is one of the largest segments of the marketing research industry and represented approximately $4 million of our revenue in 2004. Our acquisition of Rapidata met all of our criteria, as the business is immediately accretive and it expands Greenfield Online's capabilities in this significant target market. This ac-

quisition enables Greenfield Online to become the one-stop shop for health care marketing researchers with an expanded health care practitioner panel as well as a very targeted and difficult to reach patient population. We expect these added capabilities will help us accelerate the growth of our health care business segment."

We announced the acquisitions of Opinionsurveys.com, an online panel, and Rapidata on January 31, 2005. We purchased their database of panelists only; no personnel were involved with the purchase. We just added panelists.

A few weeks later on February 10, 2005, we announced the acquisition of Internet survey solutions provider Zing Wireless, Inc. (goZing) for approximately $30 million in cash, creating one of the world's largest double opt-in Internet only panels. The acquisition of goZing, a privately held Encino, California–based provider of survey sample solutions, expanded the Greenfield Online panel to 4.7 million double opt-in survey takers (1 million up on the previous number after deduplication, etc.), representing households containing approximately 12.2 million people, plus an additional 3.6 million single opt-in registrants it intended to convert to double opt-in panelists. The acquisition increased Greenfield Online's international panel by approximately 50 percent, adding more than 245,000 panel members in the U.K., France, Canada, Australia, and the Netherlands. In addition, through the goZing worldwide affiliate network Greenfield Online would have access to more than 14 million additional survey takers around the globe.

goZing's three senior executives joined Greenfield in senior management roles. Matthew Dusig, goZing's president, became SVP for Corporate Strategy for Greenfield Online; CEO Gregg Lavin became Greenfield Online's SVP for online marketing; and COO Lance Suder became Greenfield's SVP for West Coast operations. goZing had 41 employees and in 2004 recorded operating income of approximately $2.5m and revenue of approximately $13 million, 80% of which was attributable to survey sample solutions. Ten percent of the 2004 revenue was achieved through the goZing cellular reseller business, which Greenfield said was "not complementary to our current business model and was discontinued effective yesterday." The goZing client base more than doubled in 2004 to 97 clients.

Their fast growth was due to research firms looking for alternative providers, and they stepped up and became a competitive threat. go-Zing profiled respondents into specialty panels such as illness and ailments, entertainment, youth, auto, physicians, business, and IT professionals through its Techopinion.com brand. Their vertical approach was a winning strategy to get research projects and would allow us to buy those panels instead of building them and to eliminate a growing competitor. They were also headquartered in California, giving us a strong presence in the West.

I said in a press release "the transaction made sense because of the fit between the two companies' panel, people, culture and business philosophy. We are immediately strengthening our domestic and international reach, the depth of our management team, and further bolstering the capabilities of our sales and customer support staff." Matthew Dusig, goZing's president, said in the same release "it was 'a real pleasure to become a part of a company with such a powerful brand.'"

A powerful influence on our decision to buy goZing was that OTX (Online Testing Exchange) was growing rapidly and had been a big customer of Greenfield Online. We started losing some of our business from OTX to goZing. I always tried to meet regularly with our largest clients and had recently conducted a two-day meeting with Shelley Zalis, founder of OTX in London. They had been buying large amounts of sample from us at the rate of several million dollars a year at increasing rates and suddenly started to decline. OTX specialized in combining Internet tools with traditional marketing to provide strategies for the entertainment, advertising, and consumer goods industries. They were one of the fastest growing research firms in the country at that time and eventually reached $60 million in annual revenue; the company was sold to Ipsos in 2009. If it hadn't been for Shelley's advice to me about the valuable services and delivery capability of the goZing panels, I wouldn't have moved forward with the acquisition.

A few weeks later we announced our Q4, 2004 results. Revenue and "adjusted EBITDA" slightly beat analyst estimates.

Q4 Results

- Net revenue was $13.6 million, up 64% year over year, and slightly above consensus of $13.5 million.

- Adjusted EBITDA of $3.4 million beat consensus of $3.2 million, and compares to $1.4 million a year earlier.

- Gross margin 74% was up from 66% a year earlier.

- Gross profit of $10.0 million was up 83% year over year.

- Operating income was $2.5 million, up from $0.6 million a year earlier.

- Net income was $2.4 million versus $0.4 million a year earlier.

- Sales bookings, defined as newly signed contracts for online survey work, were $14.6 million, up 55% year over year and 18% sequentially.

- Bid volume, defined as the total value of online survey projects submitted for bid by clients, was $83 million, up 70% year over year and 8% sequentially.

- First-quarter backlog, defined as signed contracts for online survey projects to be completed and delivered to clients during the three months ending March 31, 2005, was $11.0 million as of February 9.

These were great results by any measure. Not to mention that during Q3 and Q4 of 2004 we went public and did a secondary offering. We also spent a great deal of time investigating potential acquisitions. These results were a credit to the management team and all of our employees. Bob, Jonathan, and I were busy executing the capital raise while Hugh, Keith, Andy, Alex, Janice, Doug and everyone else were busy adding more customers and delivering these performance-based results. An amazing year. Looking back we didn't spend enough time acknowledging what we had accomplished from where we had been a short three years ago. It was January of 2002 when we finalized the sale of our custom marketing research business; we announced these acquisitions two years later. During our earnings announcement we were supposed to explain our guidance for the current quarter. This is always a challenge for public companies. The public markets like to employ analysts to predict and study the industry and potential for future gains or losses in the stock price. For a small company like ours, with low daily trading volume the stock price is easy to manipulate.

Our Q1 Guidance, 2005

- Revenue of $15.7-$16.0 million, 83%–86% higher than 1Q '04.

- Operating income of $2.7–$2.9 million compared to $0.4 million a year earlier.

- Adjusted EBITDA of $3.8–$4.0 million compared to $1.3 million a year earlier.

- Fully taxed net income (40% rate) of $1.8-$1.9 million, versus $0.2 million in 1Q '04.

Year 2005 Guidance

- Revenues of $82–$85 million.

- Operating margins of 24%.

During Q4, 2004, we were looking at E-Rewards, Rapidata, goZing, Toluna, and Bloomerce as potential acquisitions. During our investigation of which companies would make the best additions to our global strategy, I met with Kees deJong, CEO of Bloomerce, at their offices in Rotterdam; Frederic-Charles Petit, the founder of Toluna, in London; and Max Cartellieri and Fred Paul in Munich. We were very impressed with Kees and his team. Kees was an experienced researcher and well known in Europe for his panel expertise. They were growing nicely in Europe and having a multi-lingual team in Rotterdam was appealing. Kees's research expertise and personality were a great fit for us too. Kees had co-founded Blauw Research, a custom research firm, before starting Bloomerce, which became an online panel in Europe. We were considering Toluna, Bloomerce, and Ciao as our three potential acquisitions for Europe and needed to settle on one. Survey Sample International was a competitor too at that time and actually headquartered about 20 minutes from ours in Westport. SSI started in 1977 with telephone samples for the marketing research industry. They were larger than us at that time, so we never got into serious discussions with them.

The meeting with Frederic-Charles Petit, founder of Toluna, also went well. It did seem that Toluna wasn't ready to become a part of another company. It is interesting how things played out in our industry with Toluna becoming the buyer of Greenfield Online several years later. Our first meeting with Frederic-Charles in 2004 started the relationship. I was no longer with Greenfield Online when Toluna ultimately bought Greenfield. Harris Interactive is now a part of Toluna and Frederic-Charles Petit is President. The discussions with all the potential companies were happening quickly and moving rapidly. We were actually in conversations with goZing, Rapidata, Ciao, Toluna, E-Rewards, and Bloomerce all at the same time. We were juggling our strategy and prospects. The team in Munich at Ciao did have a unique business model. The growing demand for people to respond to surveys looked to be our biggest challenge. Having the largest, best-managed panel of people globally that would respond and that we could target based on deep profile knowledge looked to be the path to establishing Greenfield Online as the global leader in online data collection. Ciao provided a platform where registered users could write reviews on a wide variety of products to help others make decisions. It claimed 26.5 million visitors per month and also provided up-to-date price comparison information from thousands of online merchants. Ciao had a technology platform, online community, and merchant relationships. They had sites in the U.K., France, Spain, Germany, the Netherlands, Italy, and Sweden. Ciao offered a comprehensive source for intelligent online shopping which combined consumer reviews and ratings of its multi-million users and the latest pricing information coming from online merchants. In Europe, it was the number one shopping platform; number one in the Spanish, German, and Italian markets; third in the Netherlands; and fifth in Sweden and the U.K. Ciao was the most organized platform where you could find user-generated content. If you wanted to buy a car, for example, you would Google a Fiat Panda for a review, and you'd likely find Ciao there. The biggest challenge was making people understand that everything's already in Ciao, all the reviews are in Ciao. Their users, since they were actively providing reviews, were willing to respond to surveys. This gave us a unique profitable way to build respondents versus having to spend money on buying panelists, like we were doing in the U.S. We saw the potential to use their platform everywhere. Our biggest expense in the U.S. concerned attracting people to join our panel. The Ciao platform was making money on the sale of items through the reviews being written. When someone read a review and clicked to a merchant to buy, Ciao made money. The merchants paid for the advertising spot and paid when an item was sold. They also made money every time someone completed a survey. This was an innovative business model that was working well in Europe. We also liked the idea of expanding our business model to additional revenue streams like ecommerce and advertisements. On April 11, 2005, we announced the acquisition of Ciao for $154 million EUR; $57.7 million was paid in cash and the rest with 3.9 million shares of Greenfield Online common stock. Extracts from the conference call discussing the deal:

> "...most of the activity is... focused in categories such as consumer durables, including digital cameras... because that is where the demand for consumer information, and also the willingness of consumers to provide such information, is highest. However... it is really just an anchoring point of our relationship with the panelists, which ends up in many cases... having more than 300 data points and consumer profile points on each one of them, including health profiles, car ownership, and other important characteristics. Everyone has cash accounts, virtual cash accounts on the Ciao site. So whenever you interact in the community and you do something that we deem worthy of remuneration, you will end up getting a few cents or a few euros for participating in things. These tend to sit on your virtual Ciao account up to the point when you press a button and request that money to be physically transmitted into your bank account, which, by the way, serves as a great way of again checking the data and making sure that we really have perfect demographic profile and address information and those kind of details."

On April 17, 2005, *Barron's* liked the move. Bill Alpert, author of the *Barron's* Technology Trader column, included a brief description of Greenfield Online in the magazine, and concluded: "The company earned 34 cents a share last year, and could earn almost 75 cents this year. It came public last July at $13, and did a follow-on offering in December. With last month's expiration of the insiders' stock lock-up, the shares have settled down to a recent 19.18—valuing the company at a bit more than $400 million, or about 21 times the consensus estimate for next year's earnings. That's not bad for a growing company in a growing business."

I resigned as CEO of Greenfield Online on September 30, 2005.

13

The Great Recession

December 2007 until June 2009 was the next major down economy to occur after the "bubble burst" in 2000 and 2001. This horrible economic downturn for the United States economy, which also had worldwide implications, is now referred to as "The Great Recession." It lasted one year and six months, and unemployment hit a high of 10% in October of 2009.

I was contacted by Chris Pacitti, who was a General Partner at Austin Ventures, sometime during the summer of 2005 while I was CEO of Greenfield Online. Austin Ventures had been following Greenfield Online and asked if I would consider leaving the company and joining the Austin Ventures "CEO in Waiting Program." Their investment concept was to find experienced CEOs and work with them to identify market opportunities and companies positioned to do well in those markets, acquire a company or two, and put the CEO in to run it. Due to my domain expertise in the online data collection industry that I had developed over the last four years, I did have a few ideas. Brands were looking for ways to reach consumers and their customers to gather feedback and conduct surveys. At Greenfield Online we were using software from Confirmit to program our surveys. We had developed our panel management software because we couldn't find anything adequate to license or use. Jeffrey Henning and Rich Nadler had started an interesting software company in Braintree, Massachusetts, called Perseus. Not only did their software enable the user to program a complicated survey, it also allowed the user to build proprietary panels of their customers or consumers to use for feedback. Jeffrey Henning actually coined the term "enterprise feedback management" that was later adopted by Gardner as an industry to analyze and cover. The idea of identifying a business to acquire, grow it, and sell it was very interesting to me—and fun. I joined Austin Ventures and identified Perseus as a potential company. I had met Rich Nadler and Jeffrey Henning while CEO of Greenfield Online. We actually investigated their products to use to help manage our panels. There was no other technology that we found that came close to their functionality.

Gartner projected that 40 percent of total feedback system deployments would be "enterprise feedback management" (EFM) solutions in 2008. I left Greenfield and began negotiations to buy Perseus with Austin Ventures in October of 2005. It is worth noting that the motivation to pilot/deploy EFM is often to reduce the reliance on (or reduce the costs of) traditional satisfaction research.

Esteban Kolsky, when a research director at Gartner, described the market structure as follows: "The market for these tools is a highly fragmented one, with no single provider. It's going to jumpstart a bunch of acquisitions as larger vendors look to work EFM and surveying into their growth strategy." Since then, technology companies such as Medellia and Satmetrix have received significant backing from venture capital investors, and the EFM market grew 60% to 70% in 2005 and 2006.

In recent years, EFM solution providers have focused on rounding out their capabilities to conduct surveys across multiple deployment modes: email, website, phone, IVR, SMS, paper, fax, and kiosk. The next generation of EFM solutions also enable companies to capture feedback from critical new sources including social media, online communities, call recordings, contact center notes, and more, to get a true "360-degree view" of the customer. The ability to monitor feedback via social media has become increasingly important, as ever-growing numbers of customers are sharing their views via blogs, Facebook, Twitter, news sites, forums, review sites, and video sites. With the help of responsive touch point tracker software, it is also possible to receive reliable feedback directly at points of sale. As a result of mobile friendliness, the feedback can submitted through both tablets and smartphones.[18]

Chris Pacitti, David Lack (from Austin Ventures), and I worked closely together to define the potential acquisition targets. In addition to the market opportunity we wanted to find a good software platform, and if it was a licensed software solution, we wanted to convert it to a SaaS model. Having just done multiple acquisitions, it was easy for me to get a dialogue going with Rich Nadler to see if he would be willing to sell. One of our criteria was to find companies that were majority owned by individuals. We wanted the negotiations to move quickly and to keep them simple. We not only negotiated cash for the owner upon the closing of the purchase, but we wanted them to continue to work at the company. In addition to a salary and bonus we gave stock options in the new entity.

Another example of determining a verifiable sales strategy was how we did it at Vovici. At Vovici we were developing an enterprise survey solution that allowed corporations to build online communities of their customers so they could get feedback and answers to survey questions directly by surveying them with our platform. Most of you are familiar with a company called Survey Monkey. They were gaining traction and a strong competitor based on their business model, which was to try it for free, create a limited number of questions, and send an email to your own list of people that included a link in the email to the survey you created with the Survey Monkey online tool. The cost at the time was approximately $500 per year per user with a limited number of surveys and number of people that would respond, and you could pay monthly.

The problem here is that many employees have the right intentions of getting feedback from customers. However, allowing anyone to create a survey and to send it to a list of customers has a few problems. First, the person designing the survey and asking the questions may have no experience at all in the proper method of asking a survey question. There is a science to it. The way a question is asked can cause a certain bias in the answer and the answer choices are just as important. We decided on a sales strategy to market directly to the *Fortune* 1000 companies and target the person with the title of "Voice of the Customer." In our marketing campaigns we asked "Do you know how many people in your organization are asking your customers to take surveys?" "Do you know where the data with their answers to questions resides? "Do you know how much your company is spending on survey tool software and how often your customers are being asked to answer questions?" "Would you like to know the answers to these questions for free? No catch. Just the facts."

I think you can imagine that this type of campaign would predictably be very successful. We offered valuable information to the person whose job it is to care about it, for free. We made the offer to Apple, Cisco, American Express, Marriott, and about ten others to start. After the responses and results came in, it became our standard first step in our new sales process.

This is what we found from our free survey, sent internally to all employees of these and other large organizations. On average, more than 500 Survey Monkey licenses were being paid for by individuals at their companies using their company expense reports to ask questions of their customers. At that time, Survey Monkey was small and owned by two brothers who were hosting all of their customers' surveys on servers they owned and many believed were located in their garages. Now this is just hearsay, but we couldn't find any information at the time representing where the data or answers to questions were being hosted. We also determined that most users were doing four to five surveys a year to a list they kept on their personal computers that were provided by the company. The length of the surveys was vastly different, from as few as three or four to more than 100. The experience of the survey taker was rarely considered. Rewarding the customer for answering was also almost never and perhaps truly never acknowledged. Sharing the results was not a consideration.

Imagine the results we got when we had the opportunity to present our survey results to the "Head of Customer Experience" to a

Fortune 1000 company executive. The strategy, execution, product, marketing, sales, support, and our entire team enabled our sale to be made and for us to grow. You can see by the chart below the impact this strategy and team effort had on our results.

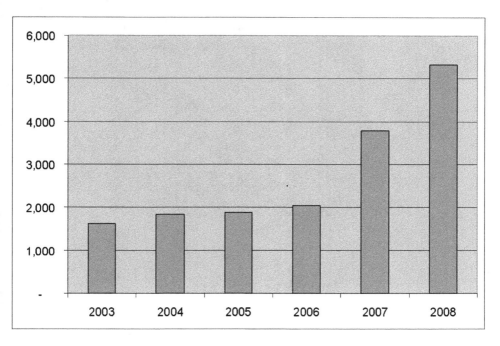

Vovici Actual New SaaS Bookings

Dean Wiltse joins as CEO December 2005

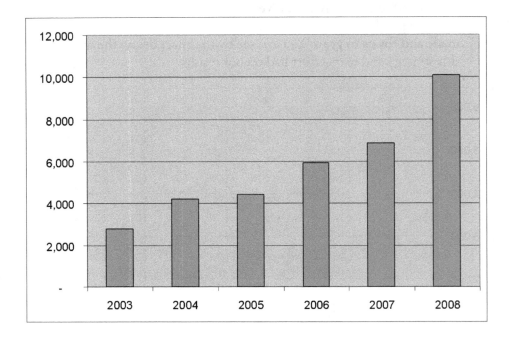

Vovici Actual SaaS Renewals

Dean Wiltse joins as CEO December 2005

Vovici Goals in '08: Accelerate Transformation into SaaS Company

1. Lessen Dependence on Services for Large Bookings
2. Increase Deals > 50k and Increase SaaS Business
3. Increase Renewable Revenue and Average Sales Price
4. Renew at Greater than 100%

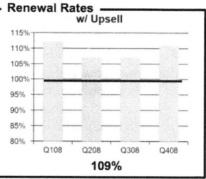

Vovici Actual 2008 Results

After the acquisition of Perseus we immediately started discussions with David Alison, Founder of Websurveyor in early 2006. David had built a great company, a competitor of Perseus, but we saw it as complimentary. Websurveyor had developed a survey tool that more directly competed with Survey Monkey, although with more functionality and at a higher price. We were impressed with the people, culture, and product of Websurveyor. We had acquired Perseus first and believed that its location in Braintree, Massachusetts, would also serve as headquarters for our newco. Websurveyor was located in Herndon, Virginia. Our thesis was that we could merge the two software codes into a single SaaS code and bring to market a solution that would address small business and departmental survey requirements, and a path to move up and across an enterprise with a sophisticated enterprise platform for customer feedback.

We closed on the purchase of Websurveyor within six months of closing with Perseus. Once we determined the overall product, sales, and marketing strategy of the combined companies, it became clear that our headquarters would need to be in Virginia. The Perseus personnel were accustomed to working remotely, but the one reservation I had wasn't having Jeffrey Henning, the co-founder of Perseus, physically located at our company headquarters. That was 2006. Today, in 2020, I think most people have become convinced that working remotely is not a drawback or limiting factor. That said, Jeffrey is a true visionary and did invent "enterprise feedback management" as an industry, and he is now Executive Director at the Market Research Institute, after serving as Chief Operating Officer at Perseus from 1993 to 2007.

We had other key contributors like Bill Parenteau, who was living in the Boston area. Bill knew everything about the product and was most likely involved in every sale and implementation at the enterprise level. Ben Smith was a sales representative selling the Perseus platform to enterprises. During the last fifteen years Ben has become a Global Vice President at Verint.

Websurveyor had created a strong process for product development, inside sales, customer success, implementation, and support. They also had a large number of customers already using their platform that would be ideal for an upsell to an enterprise solution. Brian Koma was a Vice President at Websurveyor and responsible for marketing research consulting and advice required by our prospects and customers. Jeff Beardsley was Senior Software Architect/Director at Websurveyor at the time of the acquisition of Vovici/WebSurveyor, and we soon promoted him to Vice President of the Survey Tools Group. David, Jeff, and Brian were charismatic, passionate strong leaders who managed their business with strong metrics, and it was due to those reasons we made the decision to move the headquarters to Virginia from Braintree, Massachusetts.

The year 2006 was mostly taken up with managing integration between the two companies: Perseus headquartered in the Boston area and Websurveyor in Herndon, Virginia. We had finance, marketing, sales, product, engineering, and customer success at both locations. Both companies had approximately fifty employees but duplicate positions in both cities. Unfortunately we had to navigate through those tough decisions. During that year we had to make decisions about the product roadmap and determine which code base would be the foundation of our product offering. The founders of both companies were talented technologists and so were their development teams. We had great talent in the "newco" and we had many discussions and debates about the technology and how to accomplish our goals.

Our biggest technology challenge was to move the software from a perpetual license product to a SaaS product in the cloud. Step one (while not aware that a recession was looming) was to determine our strategies, and to be sure everything was clear internally and that the entire team buys into our decisions. There are several strategies that are required in every organization. The basic questions that need to be answered are:

1. What problems are we solving
2. What markets are we in
3. What is the company vision
4. What is our sales and marketing strategy
5. What is our product strategy
6. What are our resource strategies, financial, and human resources
7. What is our employee retention strategy
8. What is our customer expansion and retention strategy

Toward the later part of 2006 we decided to make the company headquarters at Websurveyor in Herndon, Virginia. We had the people in place organizationally for engineering, QA, customer support, inside sales, research services, and our enterprise sales team was located within their sales geographies. The culture and internal processes were well managed by David Allison. We added additional CFO, marketing, operations, and customer success leadership in Herndon and focused on growing our SaaS platform sales.

14

---cΦo---

Business
Assessment

For those of you who are CEOs or considering starting your own business or becoming a CEO working for investors I would like to help you with some specific advice. As I look back at my career for the last twenty years as I have been the CEO for investors and started my own company, there are a few key things that stand out.

When I joined Greenfield Online, Vovici, and FoodlogiQ, I didn't have industry knowledge. Greenfield was a custom marketing research firm. I had been a buyer or consumer of marketing research, but I have never led a firm. Websurvey and Perseus, which became Vovici, were both perpetual software companies offering software to help conduct surveys. I had no background in SaaS when we started. At FoodLogiQ, the company was a division of a consulting services company that targeted the food industry. I had no food industry experience. I believe it was an advantage not to have specific industry experience. I could apply my decision-making skills to the knowledge I would acquire during my first weeks on the job.

When an economic downturn starts, or a global pandemic as we had in 2020, you should start an immediate "business assessment." The underlying objective is to determine how to grow and see which expenses can be cut. Get on the phone and speak to customers, not just the users but the decision makers as well. Meet and speak to your employees, especially the customer-facing ones. Meet with your IT team to understand their usage metrics. You can learn a lot from the numbers and metrics that are important for your business that have to do with the behavior of your customers. Be sure to understand where you bring value and the things that you provide that are important to your customers. In the recent pandemic, everything shut down, with managers mostly in shock as they tried to understand the impact. We began to see new messaging and services offered by companies that specifically addressed the issues caused by COVID-19. When restaurants were allowed to start opening I noticed a local popular restaurant began with signs outside indicating "we monitor our employees daily and deliver to your car window." They would accept cash-only credit cards, and employees would be required to wear gloves and masks. Airlines began by selling every other seat and talked about new methods of cleaning. New strategies were considered in every industry to survive, sustain, and then grow. They understood that in order to start growing revenues again they would need to overcome a new concern, a concern that became paramount due to the pandemic: your employee's health.

During 2001, in the midst of the early 2000s recession, I began my first days and weeks meeting almost every employee individually and called the highest level I could reach with our customers. The conversation was very similar with customers and employees. Where do you see value in the products we offer? What other areas or solutions would make sense for us to explore? At Greenfield Online the answers came quickly and consistently. We had the best online panel of people who would respond to surveys. Our method of collecting feedback online was faster, better, and cheaper than the way most surveys were being conducted at the time, which was by telephone or in-person surveys. Due to this time spent listening and interviewing customers and employees by me, someone without a biased perspective would be in a position to assess the data and make strategic decisions.

During my time at Vovici, I performed a "business assessment" in much the same way. I spoke to customers and employees to understand where they see value in our products. What else could we be doing? SaaS was new at that time. I also had to learn about the key benefits to an organization for using hosted solutions versus installed on premise software. The important takeaway for me from those conversations helped me to make important decisions about sales and marketing strategies, which enabled us to scale quickly. Survey Monkey was becoming very popular. It was an inexpensive and easy-to-create online survey that got the people you wanted to hear from: send an email with a link to your online survey created on Survey Monkey. It was a beautiful new method for getting feedback from your members, customers, and any group.

When you first heard about Survey Monkey or got an email invitation to a survey to respond your reaction was most likely, this is pretty cool. It is. However, for an enterprise this could become problematic. When I first spoke to a training manager at Cisco who was using Perseus for surveys sent to people that attended training, they loved our capabilities but wished we were less expensive, like "Survey Monkey." We asked for an introduction to the vice president of "Voice of the Customer" (VoC) at Cisco. They were happy to make the introduction. After all, they would get exposure to senior management and display their good work. I learned from my conversation with the VP of VoC that he would like visibility into the surveys conducted with *all* their customers, not just when they went through training. It would also be nice to know they went through training, took a survey, and then perhaps another survey about another topic in the future. It would be nice to see all the responses in one place so that which customers who used which products could be determined. Survey Monkey couldn't do that.

We developed a sales strategy to offer VPs of VoC of the *Fortune* 1000 a free survey of their own employees to understand how they were capturing feedback from their customers. At one *Fortune* 100 company our internal survey showed there were more than 700 Survey Monkey licenses and thousands of customers being sent surveys routinely, unmanaged across the enterprise. The license fees were being submitted on expense reports. The company was spending more than $1 million dollars per year with no understanding of how often customers were sent surveys, and their responses were not aggregated. Boom! We now knew how to make a sale into an enterprise.

Things were easier at FoodLogiQ when I started. The company was small, with only a few customers. They were not a SaaS solution and had only eight employees. Since I knew nothing about the food industry I became a sponge when listening to Andy Kennedy, one of the co-founders of FoodLogiQ and who had been with the company for thirteen years; and Jeff Ramsaur who had been with Clarkston Consulting, FoodLogiQ's parent organization, for eleven years, as a food supply chain expert. The company's roots were about food traceability, but our largest customer, Whole Foods was using our platform to manage their produce suppliers. I learned quickly through industry experts and customers that traceability was a "vision" and to implement was very complicated and costly. There were also very specific cost constraints for food distributors to implement traceability. A new label would need to be added to the food item at harvest, scanned throughout the movement in the supply chain. One President of one of the largest food distributors in the United States told me they had done an assessment. If they were to implement traceability, their truck drivers would do fewer routes, and their warehouse people could move fewer pallets around thereby making labor costly. In addition, the cost of label printing and technology made it all prohibitive.

Based on this information, we were able to develop our product roadmap and sales strategy to make "traceability" the vision, and we encouraged brands to use our platform to help them manage suppliers to be safer and compliant with their requirements. We went on to build product modules for supplier management, quality incident reporting, recall management, and traceability. During the next three years we added over fifty brands as customers such as Chipotle, Subway, Chic-Fil-A, Five Guys, Panda, Dave and Busters, Tropical Smoothie Cafe, Sweet Greens, Cava Grill, Hain Celestial, and Tyson Foods.

Recently, I was consulting with a software company that had been in business for more than ten years and was known for having a solid software platform for complex audit requirements. One particular client is a large franchisor in the food industry that uses their product to send auditors out to their franchise locations and conduct brand compliance audits. They are also widely used in the hospitality industry for the same types of applications, auditing facilities to ensure brand compliance. Every industry was hit by the pandemic and businesses came to a standstill. I was engaged to help the company get their revenues growing again so the investors could sell the business at higher valuations. Before we could establish a strategy to go aggressively after new sales in this COVID-19 recession, the company began to recoil from the impact of losing their customers. People stopped traveling, going to restaurants, and staying in hotels. What we learned was that consumers wouldn't be back until lockdowns were lifted and companies could assure their customers they would be safe. Their auditing platform could be used to validate customer and employee health with an understanding of the new cleaning protocols while communicating to their customers that they had the technology to verify health and training protocols. Business came back.

15

Getting On The Bus

Now that you have your business assessment underway and have clarified your vision, get everyone in the bus. Investors, employees—and then prospects and customers. Everyone needs to understand how your company is different and the value you bring. Depending on the size of your company or area of responsibility it is important to do a gut check about this topic especially when an economic downturn is happening. You and your key contributors should be able to easily articulate the vision for the company and what makes you different. Then, align everyone's compensation. Seriously, this is so important. You want everyone fully aligned on the vision and there is no better way to make it clear then to set objectives and performance metrics around compensation. This makes your job so much easier.

I recently went through this exercise as a consultant for a software company. The private equity firm had purchased the business six years ago from the founders and had no experience with SaaS businesses.

The beauty of a SaaS business model and the reason investors typically assign a higher value to these businesses is because with annual renewable contracts the revenue is stable and predictable. When you retain your customers and build your product to add capabilities you have a built in method to grow revenues by selling more to your customers. Those familiar with SaaS businesses understand that customer success and satisfaction are essential. In their situation they had no incentive plans for anyone to receive compensation for retaining or growing their customers. In fact, their employees had adopted an attitude with the view that certain customers were too demanding. Imagine.

I'm a big fan of incentive compensation across the organization and ownership when possible. The best method for defining a clear vision is to articulate it with compensation. Everyone in the company should have a bonus, commission, and stock awards tied to specific and clearly and openly discussed objectives. Everyone should know how everyone across the company is incentivized and how well they are doing against the goals.

Conducting this "getting on the bus" exercise is good to do on a regular basis, whether you have come in as a new manager, a CEO, or have purchased a business. Create a leadership group of managers, either selected by you or by title, but leaders from across the company with the sole purpose of defining your new vision and mission. Yes, hundreds of books are written on that topic alone. In my experience the best thinking comes from you and your team. This exercise will bring you together and begin to create that all-important team to survive whatever the world throws at you. Remember, we are reacting to a change in the business climate and need to respond quickly, so going through an elaborate process to determine your vision and mission isn't just practical or useful but necessary under unique circumstances.

I've met with Amazon on several occasions. At a couple of companies I worked with we hosted our software in the cloud at Amazon. During a meeting with Amazon to explore a partnership I was asked by the leader at Amazon Business Services to prepare a written document describing my thoughts around the partnership. He went on to say that the company had adopted using Word documents for internal discussions and proposals instead of using PowerPoint slides. I did as he asked and became a fan of the process. Initially I had a bunch or questions and you will too if you give it a try. Here are the answers to common questions:

How many pages? That's up to you. Just get your important thoughts on paper so everyone can come to the meeting prepared. We will circulate the document to everyone attending the meeting and they will be asked to read it or not participate.

Is there a structure you would like us to follow? Keep it brief. Define the objective or purpose of the paper. Define the resources needed as well as the timing and desired outcome.

What else? Your call.

This method helps everyone think their ideas through before taking up valuable time for many people in a meeting. Typically you will want to begin this process immediately. You are under the gun and time is wasting. I usually tell everyone that it is our goal to determine three to four key initiatives that we will want to consider and to make a final decision within days. This impacts people differently. Some will question the viability or quality of any decisions made this fast. Some view it as hastily made due to the timeline. I like this approach, especially if you introduce yourself to everyone and show your decisive style. Assign research or metrics as needed to make sure your decisions are well considered and then plan smaller group meetings to further discuss the ideas.

At Greenfield Online we conducted a "Getting on the Bus" meeting and as a result uncovered these game changing ideas:

The River. We needed to attract more people to join our panel and answer invites to take surveys. How could we do this at lower costs? *Answer:* We convinced Microsoft to allow us to put a link on the home page of MSN.com this "Be Heard. Give your opinion. Earn rewards." We only paid for people who took a survey and joined our panel. This seems simple today, but this helped to change an industry forever.

Company Bonus Criteria—Two Elements: Every employee in the company could earn an annual bonus of 10% of their base salary (sales people not included):

- Element 1: Growth of new revenues to existing customers. If we achieved 120% aggregated growth of revenues with existing customers, everyone earned 5% bonus annually.

- Element 2: Achievement of reaching a new bookings target when acquiring new customers; 5% bonus annually if a new customer bookings target is exceeded.

Ask yourself: If your company or area of responsibility would attain those two elements, whereby 120% revenue growth occurred for existing customers and, as a result, exceeded your new bookings targets, how would you feel? What would your business be worth?

This creates regular conversations across the company and unites the culture on specific metrics. It adds clarity to your vision and mission and helps to facilitate the right conversations and decision measurements.

At Vovici we uncovered our primary sales strategy. We had strong usage of our products within the enterprise because of our capabilities, but to make it easy for users to get quick feedback, Survey Monkey was a better alternative and inexpensive. We understood the advantages when using Survey Monkey and we also knew the advantages for using Vovici at the enterprise level. Once we got in with a sale at a department of a large organization we implemented a strategy to offer a free internal survey to our customers. Even new prospects were interested in an internal survey to determine how often someone at their company asked or sent questions to their customers and what methods they were using. Once we had those answers we were armed with actual data to support privacy, security of your customer lists and relationships, and what was being spent on tools to gather this feedback.

16

Marketing and Metrics

For those of us that have been around for some time, we are thrilled to see that marketing is metric driven today. Campaigns of days gone by never had the clear metric-driven results that we have available to us today. Buying behaviors have changed dramatically too.

If you know the questions to ask, you can quickly ascertain how well your company is doing with today's marketing techniques. If you don't know what questions to ask, I highly recommend that you learn what likely needs to be asked and considered. Every CEO needs to understand how buyers make decisions and how to reach them.

Reopening during and after the pandemic or after any economic downturn is fraught with challenges but laden with opportunities. For marketers, it's an ideal time to take advantage of new marketing and communications approaches to differentiate your brand for the "new normal" in your industry. Content is king, and now more than ever you have so many choices for getting your message out. You need to engage your customers and prospects and become a deliverer of knowledge. I am extremely proud of the accomplishments at FoodLogiQ. The company had been in business for over ten years when I arrived. Those who know the company will say the best thing that ever happened to FoodLogiQ marketing was Katy Jones, and they would be correct. My first days were in July and I hired Katy by the end of August. We had a part-time person managing the Web content and who moved a booth from one show to another with no budget, no product, and no strategy.

Katy is a student of the latest marketing techniques and managed to prove to investors we knew what to do with marketing spend and convinced them to give us a budget. Six years after Katy joined as the single marketing employee she now leads a team that has established FoodLogiQ as an industry leader. She has created and sustained strong annual growth and exceeds industry standards for customer retention. In the beginning we would meet weekly and then monthly to review key metrics that we established to be important. First and most obvious with any company is the traffic coming to your site. Eventually you will be able to monitor quality of traffic based on the number of visitors that convert to a lead and close, where they come from, what white papers were downloaded, what webinars were attended, etc. This content strategy is critical to defining your brand and the ultimate key for driving new revenue and growing current customers. Whatever you're selling just know the buyers are searching first. You need to be found first and be prevalent everywhere they search. That's it. You need a strategy and resources to pull off that objective: Know what your buyers are searching for and be prevalent at every result. Once you have defined that key list of targeted words, now you can develop your content strategy.

I have to say that this may be the most fun you will have as a CEO or leader. Our daily lives are surrounded with examining results and establishing better ways to execute across the business. Defining the right keywords for what buyers are searching for and then seeing the ranking of those words improve each week is fun. What's more, you get to witness results quickly so that you can tweak, improve, and grow more.

I have always been fortunate to surround myself with smart, intelligent, driven, team-oriented people with high integrity. As I recount my experiences as a leader from Greenfield Online, Vovici, Thumbspeak, and FoodLogiQ, my best decisions were the people I trusted and put in positions who would have a great impact. I didn't always hire the individuals, but I made the judgment calls at the time as to which roles may be best suited for certain individuals. As an entrepreneur you must always act fast. I made decisions swiftly, and the ones involving the people that would help run the company were usually the right ones.

As a first-time CEO when joining Greenfield Online, my first and easiest decision was Bob Bies, CFO. I wrote about Bob earlier. I needed to be able to rely on my CFO, trust his judgment, and respect his opinions. We didn't always agree, but since we worked together I have worked with five other CFOs, and Bob was the best. Bob had a set of skills I just didn't have. Not only was he a skilled and well-trained CPA, he had worked with investors on a Board of Directors and was used to preparing the types of information they would want to see each month. Not just profit and loss statements and balance sheets—CEOs should know how to read those—but cash flows, burn rates, runway, revenue per employee, cost of acquisition for a new customer, lifetime value of a customer, just to name a few. Learn how all of the metrics for each department are developed and rely on your CFO to help you understand the full picture of your business. Have this data and knowing what it means will help you to make better decisions.

17

Sales Leadership

I f you want to be a successful CEO you must figure out how to sell. Top-line growth is the single most important factor of the valuation of your business. Now, before you skeptics jump all over this last statement, allow me to explain. There are varying stages in a company life cycle where the rate of growth and profitability matter differently to investors. The type of business and industry are also key criteria. I don't think anyone would disagree that if your business has rapid growth and user adoption, your business is valuable. You also need to change the way you think when you hear the word "sales." Sure, you have a sales leader who manages a team of people who generally manage contacting prospects and customers and hopefully leading them to the conclusion to buy something or more. But that is just a step along the way in a process that culminates in a "sale."

I have come to know and believe that a company executes best when it is fighting for survival, like most companies do at some time during their existence. Learn to listen to customers and be sure to understand their needs. Determine sales strategies that work. That is no easy task or simple formula except that it must be explored continually. Usually a verifiable method of proving a return on investment works. I explained how we did that when we offered to take the survey results from a recently conducted telephone survey where the prospect had completed and fielded the exact same survey to our online panel. Once we gave them the results and they could truly verify that we were making factual statements, it gave them a reason to buy, which was a faster, less expensive method of doing research. Once a strategy like that is known to work it is time to develop a content marketing strategy that will drive inquiries. Create white papers with prospects that tried this method and publish the results. Publicly announce every customer win and use your targeted keywords in everything you publish.

Others would say your business is valued on EBITDA and revenues. This would be true if your top-line growth rate and user adoption rates were not high. It will be a lower valuation, but certainly a business with strong profit and revenues is worth a lot. Investments may need to be made in all areas of the company to sustain the growth; the customer success team needs different resources for training and implementation; marketing needs to cover new market opportunities for new customer acquisition; products need product managers to define what products to build next; and QA and dev ops all need to scale. Don't forget that as you add more to the team you need HR and better benefits. Strong top-line growth with controlled and logical expenses brings high valuations. It is much easier to attract investment at good valuations with strong top-line growth.

My first exposure to salesforce.com was early on in its existence. I knew I needed a tool to help manage the sales team process and marketing metrics. At that time most companies were using a software solution installed on every computer. The cloud idea came into existence because SFDC made it useful, secure, and affordable.

We used to conduct weekly company meetings that everyone could attend. Since we grew to be global we had dial-in conference meetings and screen sharing so everyone could participate in our weekly company meetings. We also recorded them because the time zones didn't always work for everyone. We did this every Monday and everyone could join and just listen in. The meetings were kept brief and usually never exceeded an hour. The purpose was for the team leader to update the status of every project underway for customers and for the sales team to talk about impending opportunities. Each of the senior managers, including me, would provide an update on our priorities. This communication helped keep everyone in the company in tune with our priorities, challenges, and key knowledge of what was important to the company. Having this knowledge empowered everyone to understand what we were doing, why we were better, and why our customers were buying from us.

Our CFO, Bob, guided the meetings by using salesforce.com dashboards and other reports that not only provided the updated information for everyone to see, but it communicated the key metrics that were important to the company. These meetings kept everyone informed and in sync about what was going on weekly at the company, and I have implemented salesforce.com within weeks of every company I joined as CEO.

Developing, implementing, and managing a sales process is essential to growing sales. Fortunately the technology tools have gotten better so that automation on many steps of a sales process can be executed based on the behavior of a prospect or customer. It is these steps that need to be identified and tweaked as results are measured. I attribute most of my success to being able to ascertain a product and sales strategy, define logical steps to move a prospect through the buying cycle, and establish sales-process metrics that can identify strong and weak areas for acceleration or improvement. I described the sales strategies we used to convert the marketing research industry from telephone data collection to online by offering to use the exact same telephone survey and field it for free to our online panel. We knew that when we got the opportunity to run this "test" they would buy. We could deliver the results in 24 hours (telephone surveys would take weeks), and if we were to charge them, our cost would be half of what they paid for the telephone survey—and the results would be the same. Now we needed a sales process to get marketing research firms to agree to give us their last telephone survey project. Picking up the phone and calling research firms cold is no longer a viable strategy. Cold calling for any sales strategy nowadays should only be done if the salesperson isn't getting enough warm leads; after all, they need to hit their number.

Marketing today is a dream because you can see results immediately. We can identify people by industry and by title on LinkedIn and

Facebook and offer up content advertisements for them to click to find out more. For example: "Reduce your survey field time to 24 hours at half the price. Click now." Once clicked they will discover content with examples of testimonials from other research firms telling about their experiences with similar results as telephone, with completion within 24 hours and at half the cost. There on that landing page they can request more information, download a whitepaper, or attend the next live webinar discussing this topic with an actual research firm. There the offer was *free* to give us their last telephone-survey project. This is a sales process that requires measurement and reporting to determine effectiveness. How many people clicked on the LinkedIn ad and completed a form that converted to a lead? Based on the investment for the ad, what is the cost to lead? How many leads converted into a free trial? How many purchased their next project from us? After a few months you have the metrics to determine if you should step on the gas and spend more to get leads. We did, and our next step was buying webinars with the research organizations to build more awareness and traffic. Our results speak for themselves: strong profitable growth during a recession.

We did it again at Vovici and FoodLogiQ. You can do it with you at your company too.

18

─────⌐❧⌐─────

Customer
Success

Sometimes known as the "voice of the customer", I like putting customer success at the forefront of every employee's mind. I like having every employee getting a bonus when the company attains significant growth from existing customers in aggregate. Everyone is an ambassador and should relish the opportunity to speak to customers and make them smile. I once advocated that every employee spend one night at a Four Seasons with an assignment of writing down everything they witnessed as a Four Seasons customer. This may not be practical, but I nevertheless recommend creating an exercise to recognize the many and easy tasks that can be done by every person at every company to be sure your customers *love* doing business with you.

Did you know that the housekeeping staff is trained to keep their carts out of the way in the hall ways and when they hear a door close in the hall they are instructed to rush out of the room they are servicing to greet the guest with a "good morning or afternoon" and ask if "there's anything I can do to make your stay more memorable"? Oh, and smile.

When you checked into your room did you see the envelope with your name handwritten on the front and a handwritten note inside just for you? If you stayed with children at a Four Seasons they would write your child's name on the wall in the bathroom over the bathtub with wet sponges spelling out their name with a bucket of toys as a gift. Every staff member says "hello" to you; even the groundskeepers pulling weeds outside are trained to stop, smile, and say hello.

I suggest determining metrics depending on your business that can be easily reviewed by all to measure how you are doing with your customers. Not simply a one-question survey asking if you would recommend your company because affordable technology exists that will enable you to have a single point of truth regarding your customers' interaction with you. Once you capture their email or phone number you can pull every touch point into one data source and measure their interaction with your company.

When a customer visits your website it can be logged into their data record that you have or can create it. The content they download, the call they make, the interaction with chat or a phone call all kept in one place. Just as important as the marketing content plan is your customer relationship management strategy and plan to execute to hit your 120% retention dollars from your previous year customers.

I have been fortunate to lead teams to develop customer-focus attitudes that have delivered 120% retention dollars from existing customers multiple times. It begins at the top with you. Every business should have a clear understanding on which customers generate the most revenue to the company and the ones with the most potential. A good rule of thumb is that the leadership team at most companies should be visiting in person when possible or at least on a video call quarterly to semi-annually. These meetings should have consistent agendas with important information your customer will want to review. How they use your products and how often they use them. Establish metrics with them that they will want to review. Keep in mind the users at your customer may be the "recommender" for the budget approval and the decision maker should be in your communication strategy and relationship building plan. A phone call from the CEO or Senior VP to the key decision makers of your top 20 customers is just as important as paying your electric bill. After all, customers keep the lights on and when they all grow, the value of your business soars.

The Greenfield Online S1 filing during our IPO stated:

"We derived approximately 27% of our total net revenues from two clients in the last fiscal year. If we were to lose, or if there were a material reduction in business from, either of these clients or our other significant clients, our net revenues might decline substantially.

"We derived approximately 27.1% of our total net revenues from two clients that accounted for approximately 14.5% and 12.7%, respectively. Either client may terminate or reduce its use of our products and services at any time in the future. Our top client in the last fiscal year was Taylor Nelson Sofres Intersearch, with which we had an alliance agreement requiring it to make purchases of at least $5.6 million of our products and services during that year. Taylor Nelson Sofres Intersearch satisfied this obligation and is no longer contractually required to purchase our products and services. Taylor Nelson Sofres Intersearch's parent company acquired NFO Worldgroup, Inc., which maintains and operates a large Internet respondent panel similar to our own. As a result of this acquisition, we expect the revenue we receive from Taylor Nelson Sofres Intersearch in the next fiscal year to be significantly less than last year. Our ten largest clients accounted for $13.8 million, or 53.4%, of our total net revenues for our last fiscal year. If we lose business from any of our top 10 clients, our net revenues may decline substantially."

During the following year we attained a net increase from current customers of over 120%.

Each of our top customers were assigned an executive sponsor, which would be me or one of my direct reports. We mapped our executive team to specific individuals at our customers to maintain contact and attend quarterly business reviews. For example, our CTO would stay in contact with our customer technical contact, our CFO stayed in contact with their CFO, and our sales leader stayed in touch with their customers' sales team leader so that we could jointly sell to new prospects together. We always assigned a specific strategic account owner to be fully responsible for growing business with their assigned customers. Remember, the entire customer success and support teams would earn an annual bonus that equaled 10% of their base salary if we grew our current customers in aggregate to more than 120%. Even our receptionist was on the bonus plan. When we moved to an automated phone system we provided our best customers with direct telephone numbers or cell phone numbers to call for immediate help. They were special and needed to be treated that way. We had an alarm bell ring in the open office if a customer was on hold over fifteen seconds. We identified the use cases our top customers used on our platform for their business and worked with marketing to develop specific content to be written that we knew would be of interest to them. We developed webinars, white papers for topics of interest expressed to us by our top customers during our regular meetings. When our top customers had suggestions for product improvements, and we agreed they were valid and helpful to all, we would add the capability to our development roadmap and keep them informed of the progress. If there were mockups or beta tests for the feature requests those customers were invited to participate. We knew that we had to fight for their business every day and wanted them to feel our efforts. We eventually added a "suggestion box" capability online where others could vote on the priority of an added feature. Our best customers were awarded bonus votes based on their size to influence the voting for prioritization.

To this day I maintain relationships that I was able to develop with customers in the past. I had memorable times with many of them. One New Year's Eve I was standing on the back deck of my house speaking with a very important customer. Their contract renewal was about to expire that day. We had been discussing the renewal and added usage for months with all of the proper approvals, but the "signer" was off on vacation until after the New Year. This was a significant contract for us and it meant that we wouldn't be able to report the renewal or the growth in our fiscal year results because we didn't have signature until after the first of the year. This also meant our employees wouldn't reach their bonus goals. Fortunately, due to the relationship I had developed I was able to reach senior leadership at our customer during the holiday break. They were working hard for us to get the signature, but as it turned out we got down to the last minute and we discovered the needed signer was on a cruise. At around 8 P.M. EST, I got a call on my cell phone that they were able to reach the signer and the completed document was on the way to me. People do want to help especially when they know you and others at the company. They will work with you towards common goals. Our best customers did value their relationships with us because we mutually benefited from the relationships. I was able to send a congratulatory email to everyone at the company on New Year's Eve thanking them for a job well done.

19

---◦◦◦---

Let the Numbers Guide You

I'm not a charismatic leader unlike Ronald Reagan and Steve Jobs, two of my leadership heroes. I haven't developed the skills to communicate in a public setting and inspire like they could. Most of us never will. What we can do is communicate clearly and systematically so that doubt and uncertainty never arises. Remove the fear of the unknown. If you don't, people will create a weird need fear, uncertainty, and doubt, regardless of how well things are going. There are people who naturally want to self-destruct and influence others negatively. Your constant communication can bury these negative influences. That alone can create greatness. People working in sync, solving problems, collaborating, looking forward, being creative, and having fun is motivating, and creates an environment for success and innovation. Every department should be able to establish mathematical metrics that indicate how well the company is doing in each area. Here is a list of my favorite metrics to review monthly at an all-hands meeting:

- Website traffic this month compared to the same period last year
- Number of online forms filled out asking for more information
- Total pipeline dollars by stage compared to last quarter same month and last year
- Number of service tickets submitted compared to the same time last year
- Response time to close tickets compared to the same time last year
- Number of customers logging in this month compared to the same time last year
- Amount of marketing content downloaded compared to the same time last year
- Revenue per employee compared to the same time last year

Each industry and size of your company will have different key measurements, so hopefully this is a good list to get you thinking about the key metrics all employees can watch to measure performance and to help you make informed decisions.

20

Attract Investors
or Sell

During my career I've had the opportunity to work with some of the best venture capital and private equity firms in the world. Here is my recommended list:

Insight Venture Partners
https://www.insightpartners.com/
1114 Avenue of the Americas, 36th Floor
New York 10036
Phone: 212-230-9200
Email: growth@insightpartners.com

Mayfield Fund
https://www.mayfield.com/

2484 Sand Hill Road

Menlo Park, CA 94025

T +1 650-854-5560

Elsewhere Partners

https://elsewhere.partners/

chris@elsewhere.partners

Tritium Partners

http://www.tritiumpartners.com/

1011 S. Congress Ave.

Bldg. 1, Ste. 350

Austin, TX 78704

(512) 493-4100

info@tritiumpartners.com

Openview Partners

https://openviewpartners.com/

617.478.7500

303 Congress St, 6th Floor

Boston, MA 02210

These firms have similar characteristics and are the very best at what they do. Look at the number of successful investments. If you haven't investigated potential investors before, we're here to help. During my career I have raised investment capital several times for different companies in different industries. Begin with investors who know your industry and have other investment experience in an industry similar to yours. Business models for companies are different in different industries. The areas you need to spend your investment for marketing, product development, sales, etc., are unique to your type of business. You will find it helpful if your investors have similar experiences because it can be very detrimental if they don't understand your business. Many think they know, but unless they have experienced an investment in a similar industry as your industry, I would stay away.

Each of the companies I have recommended have developed solid experiences with companies growing in similar industries and achieved multiple exits. They are there to help you and know how to deliver results.

As you grow, many situations and opportunities will present themselves and you will need experienced advisors to help navigate your choices. The more depth and experience you have on your team the better your odds are for success. From marketing opportunities to channel strategies to acquisitions, your investors can help.

Remember there is nothing more fun than success. I hope to hear from many of you sharing with me your stories of success during difficult times.

About the Author

Dean Wiltse is an entrepreneur. His business experience ranges from selling sandwiches door to door at Ithaca College campus dormitories, buying a video store for $25,000 that quickly became a franchise with 12 locations and was eventually sold, to leading Greenfield Online to an IPO. He is an expert in determining business and product strategy, sales, and marketing processes for enterprise and inside sales teams, and as CEO Dean has led eight domestic and international acquisitions with positive integrations and financial results. As CEO of Greenfield Online he led the acquisitions of Rapidata, goZing, and Ciao. As CEO of Vovici, he led the acquisitions of Perseus and Websurveyor.

Dean has successfully built four venture-backed startups, turnarounds, and targeted acquisitions with successful exits. He is best known for creating the first global interactive media and services company that collected consumer attitudes about products and services, enabling consumers to reach informed purchasing decisions about the products and services they want to buy.

Most recently, after three years at FoodLogiQ, he changed the business model to SaaS, determined the strategy for scale and growth, brought in an entire management team, grew annual recurring revenues dramatically each year, sustained renewal rate revenues at the highest levels recognized for SaaS companies, and completed a recapitalization for the original founders. The company had been in business ten years prior to Dean's arrival as a services company with little growth. Within three years after Dean's arrival the business became established as the food industry's most innovative SaaS provider of traceability, food safety and supply chain transparency solutions enabling restaurant chains, food retailers, growers, packers, processors, shippers, and consumer product companies to ensure they are providing safe and high quality food products to consumers.

Interview with Dean Wiltse

Will 2017 Be the Year of Transparency?

By Maria Fontanazza, Food Safety Tech, December 19, 2016

Food companies will focus on getting a better grasp of all levels of their supply chain.

The increasing complexity of the global food chain has also increased the complexity of traceability of ingredients. However, FSMA has made this task a critical part of the seed to fork process. More vigilance and awareness of the supply chain is an essential part of protecting consumers and the company brand, and plays in an important role in the event of a recall. In a Q&A with *Food Safety Tech* Dean Wiltse, CEO of FoodLogiQ, explains the issues the food industry is experience in this area and why transparency in the supply chain will become the new normal.

Food Safety Tech: What are the biggest supply chain challenges you see industry facing today?

Dean Wiltse: The biggest challenge we see in the food supply chain is getting beyond the "one-up and one-back" approach to supply chain management to achieve real transparency in the supply chain. Now I think more than ever consumers want to know more information about their food and 2017 is going to be the year of transparency. A year of getting beyond one-up and one-back, and beyond the four walls of the food manufacturing facility to really dig down and understand what is going on two, three, four, or five levels down the supply chain, from a safety and risk mitigation standpoint.

I also think food companies will continue to be challenged by the ripple effect of increased recalls: Sunflower seeds, flour, powdered milk. Many food companies were rocked with these recalls in 2016.

We expect these recalls to continue in scale and frequency going into 2017.

Another challenge is in the area of quality incidents—and the monitoring of those quality incidents. Oftentimes these quality issues go unchecked and it's damaging to the quality of your food—and of course your brand—as well as damaging to the bottom line.

FST: How should companies monitor and ensure that they are getting high quality product from suppliers?

Wiltse: It sounds simple, but it all starts with being aware of exactly where you are experiencing quality issues across your supply chain. At FoodLogiQ, we pull all of the quality and incident data together in our dashboard to enable food companies to know exactly which suppliers you are having quality issues with and which ones you aren't. Tracking and documenting these incidents—followed by the corrective actions—is critical. It is also important that all of the requirements and expectations are communicated openly; it makes the food supply chain safer by opening up transparency.

Customers can also use our technology to aggregate the quality and safety data into a star rating for their suppliers. Defining what is important to you from a quality and safety standpoint and aggregate that data in the software, and then assign a star rating for your suppliers. You can then use this star rating to formulate your preferred and approved supplier list.

FST: Where are the biggest disconnects in the supply chain? And how can companies rectify this?

Wiltse: Back to what the consumer is demanding: More information about their food, where it came from and what exactly is in it. Leading food brands want to provide this level of transparency to their consumers, but many are struggling with delivering this information in an authentic, real-time fashion.

Today there's technology that can deliver it to them. In order to get more granular and provide more detailed information through the supply chain, there's a cost associated with that, even down to the labeling at the grower for traceability. Many in the industry view this as an additional cost, but the leaders see this as a strategic investment and realize there is significant ROI in supply chain transparency.

FST: What are the most serious concerns surrounding FSMA and the supply chain?

Wiltse: Clearly the majority of the industry has been preparing for FSMA for several years now, getting their processes in place, if they weren't already. Where we see a significant opportunity for companies to be proactive is in centralizing their required records, safety plans, and other essential processes into one platform for their entire supply chain.

We see many food companies who may have the required documentation and corrective actions in place, but they are scattered or siloed throughout the organization, and not centralized and easily accessible when the FDA calls on you to provide that information.

Another challenge is certainly top of mind is foreign supplier verification. The wave of required verification for foreign suppliers will be significant for many companies so they must be vigilant and start that process now or risk a significant disruption to their business.

Endnotes

1   Keith Cline, Venture Fizz

2   *The New York Times* ran an editorial on December 24, 2000 "The Dot Com Bubble Bursts."

3   https://venturefizz.com/stories/boston/could-cmgi-have-been-google-boston

4   insightpartners.com/team

5   https://www.thebalance.com/what-does-nasdaq-stand-for-then-and-now-3306242

6   https://en.wikipedia.org/wiki/MSN

7   https://en.wikipedia.org/wiki/Automated_telephone_survey

8   https://www.theverge.com/2017/5/4/15544596/american-households-now-use-cellphones-more-than-landlines

9   https://en.wikipedia.org/wiki/United_States_Court_of_Appeals_for_the_Tenth_Circuit

10   "Mainstream Marketing Services Inc. v. Federal Trade Commission, U.S. Tenth Circuit Court of Appeals" (PDF). *ca10.uscourts. gov.*

11   "2009 Economic Report of the President, Box 9-1" (PDF). *georgewbush-whitehouse.archives.gov.*

12   https://www.pewresearch.org/methods/u-s-survey-research/collecting-survey-data/

13   "John Kasich's Biodata." *Fox News Channel.* December 1, 2011

14   Hunter, Glenn. "5 questions for Hal Brierley." D Magazine

15   Collins, Kendra. "E-Rewards: worth it or walk away?" Points and Pixie Dust

16   "Court Square to Acquire Research Now"

17   "Research Now SSI Rebrands yo Dynata."

18   https://en.wikipedia.org/wiki/Enterprise_feedback_management#cite_note-9